Paradise Lost
and the Modern Reader

Paradise Lost
and the Modern Reader

Thomas Wheeler

University of Georgia Press
Athens

Library of Congress Catalog Card Number: 73–76786
International Standard Book Number: 0–8203–0336–4

The University of Georgia Press, Athens 30602

Printed in the United States of America

For Betsy

Contents

Contents

Preface

When Balachandra Rajan published his *"Paradise Lost" and the Seventeenth-Century Reader*, his intention was "to reconstruct the response of an alert and qualified reader of the epic, who shared the values and interests of Milton's generation." The result was an enlightening and useful study of a poem which in many ways belongs to Milton's generation. *"Paradise Lost" and the Modern Reader* is a kind of cousin to Rajan's study.

In a strictly literal sense there is no "modern reader," though there are many readers of *Paradise Lost* in the modern world. This book attempts to interpret *Paradise Lost* in a way which is consonant with the experience of modern readers. I claim no particular authority to speak for my own age except that I am a part of it. And, having taught *Paradise Lost* for ten years to undergraduates and graduate students, I know something of their responses to it. Their reactions may be called naive or unsophisticated, but they are hardly uncritical. And while I try in the classroom to set *Paradise Lost* in its historical context, it is no part of my job to insist that students falsify their responses to the poem. My chief contention is that *Paradise Lost* does not speak to modern readers as Milton intended it to speak, and that the response of the modern reader is just as valid as the response of the seventeenth-century reader. I do not argue that the modern response is better or truer or in any way to be preferred. I simply contend that it exists and that it has a real basis in the text of the poem.

The most important fact about the modern reader of *Paradise Lost* is that he is outside the tradition of Christian humanism which is the immediate historical context of the poem. He does not, for instance, attribute any particular authority to the material from Genesis on which Milton bases his epic. It is simply a story. The fact that a character in the story is named God does not sway the modern reader to identify this character with the God of Christianity or with his own concept of God, if, indeed, he believes in God at all. Nor will he suppose that the Genesis account of the Fall of Man describes a real event. Addison gave leave to his readers to call *Paradise Lost* a divine poem. To the modern reader the term is meaningless. He will assume that a work of art must in some sense create its own truth, a truth which is contingent and limited. For the modern reader is a relativist. He will judge the truth of a work of art by measuring it against his own experience, not by associating it with a divine source. He will not expect the truth of a work of art to be moral or practical or prudential. It will simply illuminate his own experience.

Because the modern reader does not accord any peculiar authority to the biblical material on which *Paradise Lost* is based, he will demand that the poem establish its own authority. As all great works of literature do, it must speak to him directly as a human being. And it must speak to him in its own words: the text is absolutely primary. That is why my book appears to be naive in its reading of the poem. Not because the modern reader is an ignoramus who has never read anything but simply because he expects a work of literature to have its own existence and vitality.

I hope that my approach will not be construed as an attack upon historical scholarship. At its best such scholarship has always shown us how the work of a past age is of permanent human interest. And it has given us a sense of the depth and complexity of great literature, along with an understanding of how our own responses are just as affected by our place in time as were those of past readers. I have merely insisted that the modern reader cannot be a seventeenth-century reader and that his response to *Paradise Lost* deserves to be stated, not as superior to other responses but simply as a fact. And I claim that the greatness of *Paradise Lost* may be measured in part by the fact that it speaks profoundly to the modern reader.

This book owes much to Professors John L. Lievsay and Almonte C. Howell, both of whom helped me to appreciate the vitality of Milton's poetry. I am deeply indebted to Professors Robert H. West and Douglas Bush, whose sympathetic and penetrating comments were of great assistance to me in the revising of my manuscript. I must also express my appreciation to the University of Tennessee Graduate School for providing the summer grants which made it possible for me to accomplish both the original composition and subsequent revision of this book, and to the Better English Fund, established by John C. Hodges, for funds to support the preparation and typing of the manuscript.

Thomas Wheeler

Milton's Epic

I

When Walter Raleigh called *Paradise Lost* "a monument to dead ideas," he was referring to the profound changes in thought between 1667 and 1900—changes which to Raleigh cancelled out the validity of Milton's ideas and left only the grandeur of certain passages of poetry. How could one take seriously the thought of a poem which pictured a Ptolemaic universe created in seven days, a poem which presented as historically true the myth of a primitive garden? As far as Raleigh was concerned, the value of *Paradise Lost* was to be found entirely in its poetry, not in its presentation of a tenable view of the human condition. He described the poem as a "chapel-of-ease" for Milton's mind, "a monument to his own genius and his own habits of thought." Consequently "to find him at his best we must look at those passages of unsurpassed magnificence wherein he describes some noble or striking attitude, some strong or majestic action, in its outward physical aspect."[1]

When subsequently T. S. Eliot and F. R. Leavis attacked Milton's verse, there seemed to be very little left of *Paradise Lost*. Leavis was confident that Milton had been satisfactorily disposed of. "Milton's dislodgment, in the past decade, after his two centuries of predominance, was effected with remarkably little fuss. The irresistible argument was, of course, Mr. Eliot's creative achieve-

1. *Milton* (New York: Putnam, 1900), pp. 85, 153.

I

ment; it gave his few critical asides—potent, it is true, by context—their finality, and made it unnecessary to elaborate a case."[2]

For some forty years, however, Milton scholars have been elaborating a case in defense of Milton. They have defended both his verse and his thought. The sheer bulk of their work is impressive. For the purposes of our discussion, most of these scholars may be seen as belonging to one of two groups—those who study *Paradise Lost* as a historical artifact and those who are concerned with its message to a modern audience. In order to illustrate their methods and conclusions, we will examine briefly their analysis of the significance of Milton's Satan. The choice of Satan is primarily a matter of convenience: nearly everyone who writes books about *Paradise Lost* writes about Satan.

One of the most useful and sympathetic treatments of *Paradise Lost* from the historical point of view is Balachandra Rajan's *"Paradise Lost" and the Seventeenth-Century Reader*. Rajan's purpose is "to see *Paradise Lost* through the eyes of Milton's contemporaries." He states clearly the theory which lies behind his undertaking. "The ideal critic should be also the ideal reader, and his discussion of *Paradise Lost* should be related everywhere to the effect of the poem on the audience for whom it was intended." In dealing with the figure of Satan, for instance, he comments:

> When Satan appeals to "just right and the fixt laws of Heav'n," when he grounds his mandate on the ultimate nature of things, and when, in betraying overtones, he

2. *Revaluation: Tradition and Development in English Poetry* (London: Chatto and Windus, 1936), p. 58.

couples God's "tyranny" with "the excess of joy," you
are not supposed to take these statements at their face
value. Other politicians have made claims somewhat
similar, and Satan's assertions as the champion of liberty
would amuse, rather than perplex, those who were
brought up to think of him as the first liar.[3]

Douglas Bush's *"Paradise Lost" in Our Time*, like Rajan's work, relates *Paradise Lost* to the religious and moral
tradition of the seventeenth century. Bush argues that to
read the epic properly the modern reader must adjust
himself to the poem and learn to accept the values of
Christian humanism. Regarding the modern admiration
for Satan, Bush says:

> The fact is simply that the modern world has moved
> quite away from the old assumptions and doctrines of
> religious, ethical, social, and cosmic order and right rea-
> son. . . . We have much more sympathy with *virtù*,
> which is always exciting, than with virtue, which is al-
> ways smug. This instinctive response has of course grown
> the stronger as religion and morality have been increas-
> ingly sapped by romantic naturalism and sentimentalism.
> So thoroughly are we debauched by these flabby "lib-
> eral" doctrines that when we encounter an artist who
> passionately affirms the laws of justice, reason, and righ-
> teousness, the laws that grow not old, we cannot under-
> stand his high convictions and purposes and either turn
> from them in disgust or explain them away.

To help the modern reader understand *Paradise Lost*,
Bush provides a chapter entitled "Religious and Ethical

---

3. *"Paradise Lost" and the Seventeenth-Century Reader* (London:
Chatto and Windus, 1947), pp. 7, 15, 95–96.

Principles," in which he states briefly the basic concepts of Christian humanism. Clearly he regards *Paradise Lost* as "a temple of religious thought and feeling of which the modern reader has lost the key." The implications of the metaphor are that the poem can be understood only by a reader who is willing to give some measure of assent to those religious and ethical principles held by John Milton. That is to say, the poem must be understood as a product of a certain historical tradition and its genuine life is inextricably involved with its communication of that tradition. Because the modern reader probably is ignorant of the tradition, *Paradise Lost* will frequently offend him by celebrating "the Christian virtues for which modern man has had little use—humility, faith, and obedience."[4]

The effect of Bush's approach to *Paradise Lost* is to suggest that instead of judging the poem, the modern reader is being judged by it. This is precisely the point made by two scholars who may serve as worthy representatives of another school of Milton scholarship: the school which asserts that *Paradise Lost* does have a message for modern readers. Stanley Fish, fully aware of the difficulties which a modern reader faces when confronted by the religious and ethical principles embodied in *Paradise Lost*, concludes that Milton intended to make his epic difficult to accept. The reader must experience the Fall by his own falling into the traps which Milton has laid for him. The figure of Satan, appropriately enough, may cause the modern reader to fall into the sin of admiring evil. Fish draws our attention to Satan's thrilling

4. *"Paradise Lost" in Our Time* (Ithaca: Cornell University Press, 1945), pp. 66–67, 29, 87.

4

and defiant speech in Book I and to the subsequent comment of the narrator: "So spake th'Apostate Angel, though in pain, / Vaunting aloud, but rackt with deep despair" (I, 125–126).[5]

What are we to make of this comment, coming on the heels of such a splendid and vigorous declaration? Fish is willing to acknowledge the disparity between Satan's speech and the narrator's comment. But he finds that, far from being a fault, this disparity is the very essence of Milton's strategy. "The comment of the epic voice unsettles the reader, who sees in it at least a partial challenge to his own assessment of the speech. The implication is that there is more (or less) here than has met the ear; and since the only ear available is the reader's, the further implication is that he has failed in some way to evaluate properly what he has heard."[6]

The comment of the narrator recalls to us what we should have known all along—that Satan is wrong—and humiliates us by making us acknowledge our error.

> We are not warned ("Do not be carried away by this fellow"), but accused, taunted by an imperious voice which says with no consideration of our feelings, "I know that you *have been* carried away by what you have just heard; you should not have been; you have made a mistake, just as I knew you would"; and we resent this rebuke, not, as Waldock suggests, because our aesthetic sense balks at a clumsy attempt to neutralize an unintentional

5. This and all subsequent quotations of Milton's poetry are cited from *John Milton: Complete Poems and Major Prose*, ed. Merritt Hughes (New York: Odyssey Press, 1957).

6. Stanley Eugene Fish, *Surprised by Sin: The Reader in "Paradise Lost"* (New York: St. Martin's Press, 1967), pp. 5–6.

effect, but because a failing has been exposed in a context that forces us to acknowledge it. We are angry at the epic voice, not for fudging, but for being right, for insisting that we become our own critics. There is little in the human situation more humiliating in both senses of the word, than the public acceptance of a deserved rebuke.[7]

Just as Fish sees the reader drawn into *Paradise Lost* and made to reenact the fall of Adam, so Jon S. Lawry argues that the epic places its readers in direct relationship to the divine power. "Milton's stances place, characterize, and judge characters, author, and audience within the great unitary stance. Perhaps no such confluence of artistic with 'actual,' of involvement of author and audience within what Aristotle called 'action,' and of supposed first agents of reality with existent particulars, had ever before, or has ever since, occurred—not even in ritual or in Greek religio-civic drama."[8]

So, like Fish, Lawry argues that, in depicting Satan, Milton intends that the reader run the risk of falling into error:

Because the myth pulls us so irresistibly toward making Satan its sole subject, we should recall that both our stance as readers and the chosen initial matter of the poem insist that we, also—not merely the Infernal Serpent—experience the fall. As the good man Virgil conducted Dante first to the Inferno, so the good man Milton conducts us first to Hell, insisting that we taste these ashen fruits as well as those of the Paradise to come: "O taste

7. Ibid., p. 9.
8. *The Shadow of Heaven* (Ithaca: Cornell University Press, 1968), p. 19.

and see!" The narrative is *of* a myth but is *for* us. We must bear witness fully to the fatality and folly of an archetypal choice and consequence, and so—as Raphael says in his similar "epic" recounted to Adam—"beware . . . [because] to stand or fall / Free in thine own Arbitrement it lies" (VIII, 638–641). At best, we can then joyously avoid self-imprisoning error. At worst, we can sadly accept divine aid in escaping the prison. [9]

None of these critics is willing to accept *Paradise Lost* as a poem whose excellence lies solely in its poetic effects, as Raleigh saw it. Each of them takes the epic seriously, not only because of its poetry but also because it embodies ideas and attitudes which once were or still are of great importance to its readers. Yet each of them is, in some way, unsatisfying to the modern reader who wishes to take *Paradise Lost* seriously. Rajan's study sees no contemporary significance whatsoever in the epic; his attitude is resolutely historical: the reader's interest in *Paradise Lost* depends not upon its present meaning but upon its ability to embody ideas and attitudes which existed in seventeenth-century England. Bush apparently feels that the twentieth century has turned its back upon Christian humanism and is not able to appreciate or even understand *Paradise Lost*.

The studies of Fish and Lawry presuppose not only a total commitment to Christianity on the reader's part but also a willingness to value *Paradise Lost* for its statement of saving knowledge. When Fish speaks of "the truths God and Milton have proclaimed,"[10] he has effectively removed *Paradise Lost* from the domain of literature and

9. Ibid., pp. 133–134.
10. *Surprised by Sin*, p. 234.

7

added it to the canon of Scripture. Lawry concludes his discussion of *Paradise Lost* with this statement: "Beyond time, individual human choices must elect union with timeless, dynamic Idea. Because phylogeny also recapitulates ontogeny, author and audience assume the 'Grand Parents" roles. 'Answering his great Idea' (VII, 557), we continue to move in an action, yet are defined in eternity: So God with man unites."[11] Both Fish and Lawry suppose that the vision offered by Milton's epic must be seen as corresponding exactly with reality. But literary criticism must deal with art, imitation, fiction—the rendering of reality in words and images. Even with the inspiration of the Holy Spirit, Milton wrote poetry, not Holy Writ.

Unfortunately these studies do not offer a serious consideration of what *Paradise Lost* conveys to modern readers as a poetic vision of life. To be sure, they present what their authors suppose Milton attempted to show. They do this either by accepting the narrator's statements or by going outside the epic to appeal to Christian teaching. Of course, it may be asked what other way there is to read a work in which it is so obvious that the author has attempted to present a vision of the human condition according to the teachings of Christianity.

One way is indicated by E. M. W. Tillyard in his *Milton*. In a chapter entitled "Paradise Lost: the Unconscious Meaning" Tillyard begins by asserting that "a close study of the text would reveal many instances of Milton's betraying what he will not admit or does not realise he feels." Satan is an obvious example. "The character of Satan expresses, as no other character or act or feature of the poem does, something in which Milton be-

11. *The Shadow of Heaven*, p. 288.

lieved very strongly: heroic energy." God, the Son, and the angels may show strength and energy at various points in the poem, "but there is only one figure in *Paradise Lost* whose strength is shown through conflict and endurance. This is Satan, and it is through him that Milton's own heroic energy is most powerfully shown."[12]

Tillyard, in effect, argues that what one finds revealed in *Paradise Lost* is the mind and heart of John Milton. And these are revealed in a way that even John Milton did not recognize. Though he was not of the Devil's party, his presentation of Satan is such that "we are perfectly certain, in spite of all arguments to the contrary, that Satan showed a noble and virtuous energy in rousing himself from the fiery lake and inspiring his fellows with his own desire for action, the one thing that could make their existence tolerable."[13] Tillyard is willing to grant that there is something in *Paradise Lost* which cannot be accounted for either by seventeenth-century Christian humanism or the epic's capacity to provide saving knowledge.

Another way of reading the epic is provided by William Empson in *Milton's God*. Empson argues that to justify God's ways to men, Milton had to attempt a thorough rehabilitation of the Christian God. "Milton was right to feel that, in undertaking to defend the Christian God, he had accepted a peculiarly difficult client."[14] The burden of Empson's argument is that Milton was aware of the savage aspects of the God of Christianity and, consequently, sympathetic to Satan. He presented Satan in such a way as to justify his rebellion, primarily

12. *Milton* (London: Chatto and Windus, 1949), pp. 276, 277, 278.
13. Ibid., pp. 278–279.
14. *Milton's God* (London: Chatto and Windus, 1961), p. 242.

by suggesting that God forced Satan into a position which gave him no choice but to rebel.

What needs to be noted here is not Empson's conclusion but his way of reading *Paradise Lost*. He consistently discounts the comments of the narrator upon the actions or speeches of the characters. "The great line '*Who durst defy th'Omnipotent to Arms*' (I, 50) is not ascribed to one of the characters; for consistency it has to mean that, though Milton believes God to be omnipotent, Satan dared to hope he could be defeated." Instead of reading Satan's speeches as a series of lies, Empson supposes that, at least in the early books, Satan is consistently honest. Concerning the background of Satan's revolt, he comments, "We need therefore to make deductions from what the supernatural characters let drop about what happened earlier, much as we would in a play by Ibsen."[15] Certainly Empson's whole method is consistent with that remark. He reads *Paradise Lost* as if it were a play. That is why he responds as he does to the great speeches, while he explains away the narrator's comments.

Similarly A. J. A. Waldock finds a tension between the reader's response to *Paradise Lost* and what he supposes to be Milton's intentions: "My particular concern has been with *Paradise Lost* as poetic narrative, and when all is said the narrative problems are basic, for the poem is a story or it is nothing." According to Waldock we cannot like Milton's God: we see Satan deliberately manipulated and degraded by the poet; we find Adam most admirable precisely at the moment when he consents to the original sin. It is not that Milton did not know what he was doing but that the difficulties of the story were insuperable. "In

15. Ibid., pp. 37, 36.

any case the *Paradise Lost* that Milton meant is not quite the *Paradise Lost* that Milton wrote, for the *Paradise Lost* that he meant was, in a strict sense, unwritable."[16]

Now there is one point on which all these critics and scholars agree, regardless of how much they disagree about other matters: the value and significance of *Paradise Lost* must be measured by something *outside* the poem. Its ability to convey the beliefs and attitudes of seventeenth-century Christian humanism, its revelation of the mind of John Milton, its teaching of religious truth, its covert attack upon the Christian concept of God, its correspondence with what the critic thinks Milton meant to say—these are touchstones for interpretation and criticism. Waldock himself challenges C. M. Bowra for writing not about *Paradise Lost* but about "a ghost-epic shaped in our minds from what we know very well Milton was trying to do."[17] Yet Waldock is quite sure, not only that we know very well what Milton was trying to do, but also that this knowledge is a standard by which the poem is to be judged.

It seems to me that the study of *Paradise Lost* is plagued by this kind of view. How many other poems are read in this way? Who would read the *Faerie Queene* to discover the lineaments of a gentleman? Who would read the *Aeneid* for its glorification of Augustus and imperial Rome? How many readers go to the *Divine Comedy* for its saving doctrines? We turn to these poems for their art, not for their historical or doctrinal significance, not because they are monuments to dead ideas but because their living presence engages us, touches our lives. What they

16. *"Paradise Lost" and Its Critics* (Cambridge: Cambridge University Press, 1947), p. 143.
17. Ibid., p. 144.

mean to us is determined in part by what they are, in part by what we are. What their authors meant them to be is, perhaps, totally irrelevant to us. We are free to read them as we choose; indeed we can hardly read them any other way. They do not belong to their creators or to their intended audience.

The authors of the studies alluded to above, stimulating and enlightening as they are, all regard *Paradise Lost* from the point of view of what its seventeenth-century readers expected it to mean or what Christianity demands it to mean or what Milton intended it to mean. They all have the great merit of assuming that the epic does mean something, that it is not merely a collection of splendid passages. They are aware that the poem is large and complex, that it was not written for a twentieth-century audience, that at times it is difficult to reconcile one's response to the poetry with what one may suppose Milton intended or what orthodox Christianity demands. They deal with very real tensions between the poem and its modern readers and acknowledge tensions within the poem itself. My only quarrel with them is that they all attempt to deny the validity of these tensions, primarily by arguing that the reader is not capable of reading *Paradise Lost* correctly.

This, it seems to me, is to deny the perceptible tension that exists between the reader of any work of literature and the work itself, a tension that can only increase as the passage of time increases the gap between the work and its readers. We cannot read *Paradise Lost* as Thomas Ellwood or as John Dryden did. But we need not feel bad about that. After all they could not read *Paradise Lost* as we can. Besides we are alive, which, in some ways, is a great advantage. What we want from *Paradise Lost* is a vision of the human condition to which we can respond.

Nevertheless we cannot help recognizing that there are aspects of the poem to which we cannot respond as a seventeenth-century reader would have. Perhaps all of Milton's contemporaries would have agreed with the epic's estimate of Eve as inferior to Adam. Many modern readers cannot, and we may well ask whether the poem indeed shows her to be inferior. There is no denying that when we read, "Hee for God only, shee for God in him," we are quite aware of the tension between us and the narrator.

There are, of course, ways of relaxing this tension but they all have their cost. One may argue the historical case, as John Steadman very ably does.

> *Paradise Lost* will never be merely a "monument to dead ideas." Milton's own poetry will always give even the most moribund concepts a vicarious, if shadowy, life. But the poem does run the risk of becoming a ruined monument. Its integrity has been threatened again and again by critics and scholars who disregard its seventeenth-century context and substitute twentieth-century ideas for those of Milton's age. In actuality, the poetic structure and the intellectual structure are inseparable, and the poem's integrity depends largely on this "hypostatic union" of two different orders. The imitation presupposes a reality beyond itself. To dissociate *Paradise Lost* from the structure of ideas is to violate the very nature of poetry, as Milton and his generation conceived it.[18]

This is perfectly sound doctrine for historical critics. Modern readers, by and large, will find it hard to take.

18. *Milton's Epic Characters* (Chapel Hill: University of North Carolina Press, 1968), p. 13.

There is, after all, nothing sacred about "the very nature of poetry, as Milton and his generation conceived it." Not many readers will come to the poem with any knowledge of how Milton and his generation conceived of the nature of poetry. The cost of this historicism is very high: nothing less than to bar *Paradise Lost* from touching the lives of most of the people who read it today.

On the other hand, for Stanley Fish the poem not only touches our lives but points to saving knowledge: "If he has done his part, the reader is raised to an imaginative, almost mystical apprehension of what the poem has continually asserted from a thousand varying perspectives—salvation is through Christ."[19] Any tension between the poem and the reader must be relaxed by the reader's total submission to the poem. Quite apart from the fact that many readers cannot do this, we ought to ask whether salvation through Christ is indeed the central assertion of *Paradise Lost* and, beyond that, whether we wish to begin estimating the value of poems by their capacity for saving our souls.

We have a right to read *Paradise Lost* as modern readers. We may not read it as Milton intended, but if we read with as much intelligence and sensitivity as we can muster, we are not likely to outrage his shade. If his epic cannot abide our touch, of what value is it to us anyway? Joseph Summers has clearly seen our need to read *Paradise Lost* in this way.

> It is, I think, *our* great heroic poem. Perhaps some of our difficulties arise from the fact that we have seen it too exclusively as a poem which looks to the past, to an alien antiquity, and not sufficiently as one which looks also as

19. *Surprised by Sin*, p. 328

firmly and unmistakably towards the future. Perhaps, conscious of the mistakes which the Romantics made in their reading of it, we have not boldly enough taken possession of it as our own. . . .

If we recognise *Paradise Lost* as a modern poem and not merely as a last great manifestation either of a dead classical form or an outdated religion, we will no longer be able to treat it as a "sacred" object, one before which we occasionally give official genuflections almost in order to make sure that it is safe, that it cannot harm us or intervene directly in our lives.[20]

To make *Paradise Lost* our own, we need especially to lay aside any preoccupation with Milton's intentions. To read *Paradise Lost* with the nagging sense of Milton's intentions coming between us and the poem is nearly equivalent to making seventeenth-century readers of ourselves. Milton's intentions are the rocks on which so intelligent and stimulating a book as *Milton's God* founders. Empson may see the Christian religion as a regression to a pagan desire for torture and human sacrifice, and he is quite at liberty to read *Paradise Lost* as an attempt to hide the savagery of such a religion, but when he asserts that Milton recognized God as harsh and arbitrary and intended to reveal as much of the awful truth as he could,[21] we can only reply that Milton's intentions, insofar as they are clearly stated in the poem, are quite differ-

20. "The Embarrassments of *Paradise Lost*," in *Approaches to "Paradise Lost*," ed. C. A. Patrides (Toronto: University of Toronto Press, 1968), pp. 75–76.

21. "No doubt Milton would only have snorted if a Victorian had come up and praised him for making Satan good, but anyone who told him he had made God wicked would find his mind surprisingly at home" (Empson, p. 205).

ent. Similarly, when Tillyard tells us of the unconscious meanings in *Paradise Lost* (those that Milton did not intend us to apprehend), we may admire his insight, but we have to insist on reading the poem, not the mind of John Milton.

But upon what basis does a reading of *Paradise Lost* which abandons seventeenth-century Christian humanism and the intentions of John Milton proceed? How do we make the poem our own? It would be absurd to read the poem as if Christianity had never existed. It would be equally absurd to read it as if John Milton had never existed, though some scholars ask us to read it as if we did not exist. Within limits, however, it is possible to read the epic as a work of art which creates and defines its own values by making it necessary for us to respond in a manner that is suggested by its plot, diction, images, rhythms, and sounds. These elements may combine to suggest a response which we guess that Milton intended, but what is primary and paramount is the response, not Milton's intentions. Thus, if we feel that the Satan of Book I is a sublime figure toward whom we can respond with sympathy and admiration, we need not feel sinful or contrite about such a literary experience. Milton's intentions come in a poor second to our actual experience of his poem.

It can be argued that such a method is anarchic or solipsistic. If every man is allowed to read the poem this way, who can foresee what interpretations will be formulated? What would John Milton say? Fortunately we know what John Milton *did* say about a matter not totally unrelated to this. In the preface to his *De Doctrina Christiana* Milton asserted the necessity of an individual response to the Scriptures:

But since it is only to the individual faith of each that the Deity has opened the way of eternal salvation, and as he requires that he who would be saved should have a personal belief of his own, I resolved not to repose on the faith or judgment of others in matters relating to God; but on the one hand, having taken the grounds of my faith from divine revelation alone, and on the other, having neglected nothing which depended on my own industry, I thought fit to scrutinize and ascertain for myself the several points of my religious belief, by the most careful perusal and meditation of the Holy Scriptures themselves.

If therefore I mention what has proved beneficial in my own practice, it is in the hope that others, who have a similar wish of improving themselves, may be thereby invited to pursue the same method.[22]

John Milton believed in the liberty of all men to interpret the Scriptures. It is hard to see how a man who held that belief could oppose the honest liberty of modern readers who wish to read his epic with the same kind of freedom. I submit that a truly Miltonic reading of *Paradise Lost*, one best fitting the spirit of John Milton, is a reading which tests the poem instead of accepting the received orthodoxies, Christian or Miltonic. Such a reading will depend on the letter of the text, just as Milton's treatise adhered "to the Holy Scriptures alone."[23] Without regarding the poem as a sacred text, it will assert that the poem must be true to itself before it can be true to

22. *The Works of John Milton*, ed. Frank Allen Patterson, 18 volumes (New York: Columbia University Press, 1931–1938), XIV, 5.
23. Ibid., XIV, 15.

anything outside itself: that is, the primary truth of *Paradise Lost* is *in* the poem.

To read *Paradise Lost* this way does not imply any hostility toward other ways of reading it. Historical scholarship has performed an immense service for the readers of the poem. It has shown us that Milton's epic is a product of a great tradition. It has enabled us to see exactly how Milton used that tradition and how he went beyond it. It has given us a sense of the tremendous resonance of *Paradise Lost*, its capacity to respond to and give new force to both classical and Christian thought and literary art. For this great achievement modern readers may quite properly be grateful. Nothing in this study implies a rejection of historical scholarship.

Even though *Paradise Lost* is a product of a great historical tradition, it is also a part of the modern reader's experience. And in many ways his experience is significantly different from that of a seventeenth-century reader. To argue that the modern reader may benefit from an interpretation of *Paradise Lost* which is based on twentieth-century literary values and responses is not to reject historical scholarship. It is rather to insist that the continuing life of the poem depends upon its ability to address itself to its readers, not only as a revelation of Christian teaching but also as a vision of the human predicament, a vision with its own special qualities and emphases, not precisely identical with any particular version of Christian orthodoxy. In the course of justifying the ways of God to men it must also justify itself to us.

The Voices

2

In her sensitive and helpful study, *Milton's Epic Voice*, Anne Ferry asserts that for *Paradise Lost* Milton had to develop a special kind of narrator: "his story, because it is 'invisible' to us, demanded not only a narrator but one endowed with unique powers of vision to make the impenetrable world of prehistory known to us. It is his voice, as we shall see, which interprets the story to us, and which is the principal device in the poem for expressing its *total* meaning."[1]

Her analysis of this narrator's role appears to be, at least in part, a response to those criticisms of *Paradise Lost*, like Waldock's, which emphasize a discrepancy between the reader's reaction to events in the poem and the comments of the narrator. Perhaps the best example occurs in Book IX, when Adam completes the original sin:

> he scrupl'd not to eat
> Against his better knowledge, not deceiv'd,
> But fondly overcome with Female charm. (IX, 997–999)

Concerning this passage, Waldock has written:

> We have here, I would suggest, a perfect illustration . . .
> of the sort of clash that we must sometimes expect in
> *Paradise Lost* between Milton's theory of a matter and
> the matter as he has actually presented it. This is, indeed,

1. Anne Davidson Ferry, *Milton's Epic Voice* (Cambridge: Harvard University Press, 1963), p. 15.

one of *the* moments in the poem for bringing that distinction to bear. "Fondly overcome with Femal charm" is simply Milton's comment on the recent course of events: events the true nature of which he has just been demonstrating to us. And between a comment and a demonstration . . . there can never be real question, surely, which has the higher validity.[2]

To deal with this kind of discrepancy, Mrs. Ferry wishes to establish a sense of rapport between the reader and the narrator "whose identity and characteristic tone are sustained throughout the epic and control our interpretation of its meaning." This narrator is not John Milton; he is an inspired bard who "can interpret to us Adam's story and our own share in it because, like a bird, he can soar beyond the limits of our mortal experience and our fallen vision." The narrator, because he is both a fallen man and an inspired bard, has a "double point of view" deriving from "his fallen knowledge and his inspired vision."[3]

To this inspired narrator Mrs. Ferry attributes a kind of absolute authority. Where there is apparently a discrepancy between our response to what a character says or does and the narrator's comment, "we must judge the character by the interpretation, not the interpretation by the character's words or acts." One might wonder why this is so. She explains: "We cannot judge the characters simply by their values in relation to our own because the unfallen world of prehistory in the poem cannot be measured by mortal imaginations."[4] This would seem to

2. *"Paradise Lost" and Its Critics*, p. 49.
3. *Milton's Epic Voice*, pp. 22, 24, 56.
4. Ibid., pp. 16, 15.

grant a new kind of immortality to the narrator of *Paradise Lost*, whether we identify him with John Milton or not. It suggests that the narrator has an authority which many modern biblical scholars would be loath to attribute even to the Holy Scriptures.

Everything in the epic comes to us through the medium of this narrator. "Nothing takes place in the poem which is not first spoken, or heard and retold by the narrative voice."[5] That "first" might lead to some intriguing speculations, but our concern lies in another direction. For Mrs. Ferry implies that we are everywhere and always conscious of the narrator, as if we were reading "Spotted Horses" and hearing the characteristic accents of V. K. Ratliff. There are passages that she does not refer to that suggest another sort of narrator, one who can react strongly and positively to the values of fallen mankind. For example we are carried along through a great part of Book I by a voice which conveys a sense of heroic energy, fierce defiance, and bold design. Not only the speeches of Satan but the narration of events in Hell show this positive response to the fallen angels. That voice speaks to us in these lines:

> All in a moment through the gloom were seen
> Ten thousand Banners rise into the Air
> With Orient Colors waving: with them rose
> A Forest huge of Spears: and thronging Helms
> Appear'd, and serried Shields in thick array
> Of depth immeasurable. . . .   (I, 544–549)

This is a voice which expresses magnificence, a sense of magnitude, and the exhilarating pressure of united, de-

5. Ibid., p. 45.

fiant action. It is the same voice in which Satan addresses his legions, giving them new hope:

> Powers and Dominions, Deities of Heav'n,
> For since no deep within her gulf can hold
> Immortal vigor, though opprest and fall'n,
> I give not Heav'n for lost. From this descent
> Celestial Virtues rising, will appear
> More glorious and more dread than from no fall
> And trust themselves to fear no second fate. . . . (II, 11–17)

The same voice tells us how they built Pandaemonium:

> Soon had his crew
> Op'n'd into the Hill a spacious wound
> And digg'd out ribs of Gold.   (I, 688–690)

But then follows a comment:

> Let none admire
> That riches grow in Hell; that soil may best
> Deserve the precious bane.   (I, 690–692)

One is tempted to ask, who said that? Surely this neat, rather prim aside is not spoken by the narrator of Hell's magnificence. In the midst of this splendid narrative another voice has broken in, speaking in perfectly regular iambics which contrast with the tough vigor of the preceding "digg'd out ribs of Gold." It is a voice of admonition, of denial, and it contrasts briefly but strongly with the lines that precede and follow it.

Now it is quite possible to associate gold with dross, to portray magnificence as outward show contrasting with true worth. Milton does this often. But we are not prepared for this vision in Book I. In the atmosphere of heroic energy and gloomy splendor, the prudent voice of the moralist is strangely out of tune.

Just as oddly out of tune is the voice of God in Book III. Hardly any passage in *Paradise Lost* is as harsh as that in which God proclaims his mercy towards mankind. J. B. Broadbent has noted the similarity between "the Father's rhetoric in Book III and Satan's."[6] God and Satan speak in nearly the same voice at times. There is a certain quality of hard assertion building up to one final succinct declaration that is heard again and again in their utterances. As in Satan's

> Here we may reign secure, and in my choice
> To reign is worth ambition though in Hell:
> Better to reign in Hell, than serve in Heav'n. (I, 261–263)

The same voice is heard in God's pronouncement:

> This my long sufferance and my day of grace
> They who neglect and scorn, shall never taste;
> But hard be hard'n'd, blind be blinded more,
> That they may stumble on, and deeper fall;
> And none but such from mercy I exclude. (III, 198–202)

Eve presents another example of a voice that is, if not out of tune, at least so rapidly modulated as to shock the ear. Many critics have felt the charm of Eve's exquisite lyric in Book IV. But one must note also its abrupt, discordant conclusion.

> Sweet is the breath of morn, her rising sweet,
> With charm of earliest Birds; pleasant the Sun

6. *Some Graver Subject* (London: Chatto and Windus, 1960), p. 150.

When first on this delightful Land he spreads
His orient Beams, on herb, tree, fruit, and flow'r,
Glist'ring with dew; fragrant the fertile earth
After soft showers; and sweet the coming on
Of grateful Ev'ning mild, then silent Night
With this her solemn Bird and this fair Moon,
And these the Gems of Heav'n, her starry train:
But neither breath of Morn when she ascends
With charm of earliest Birds, nor rising Sun
On this delightful land, nor herb, fruit, flow'r,
Glist'ring with dew, nor fragrance after showers,
Nor grateful Ev'ning mild, nor silent Night
With this her solemn Bird, nor walk by Moon,
Or glittering Star-light without thee is sweet.
But wherefore all night long shine these, for whom
This glorious sight, when sleep hath shut all eyes?

(IV, 641–658)

Eve's lyric is full of the sweetness and bliss of Paradise. Her question mars the music of her song. Much has been made of Eve's dream as a foreshadowing of the Fall, even as a fall itself. Adam's voice absolves Eve of guilt for her dream, but who will absolve her of this strangely discordant curiosity? Of this fall from the height of lyric sweetness and grace to the level of mere inquisitiveness? Do we not hear in Eve's voice something of that triviality of mind that Tillyard found in her deliberations before the Tree of Prohibition?[7] Or that lightness which we hear again in Book IX when she says to Adam, "On my experience, *Adam*, freely taste, / And fear of Death deliver to the Winds" (IX, 988–989). What a breezy utterance that is!

Adam's voice is not like Eve's. His is the accent of grav-

7. *Milton*, p. 260.

ity and earnestness. If Eve wants to know why the stars
shine all night, he will answer soberly and seriously. God
may tease him, but Adam's requests are patiently persis-
tent. Like a good pupil he receives his lessons from Michael. Just as Eve's fall is prefigured by her voice in Book
IV, Adam's fall is implicit in Book VIII as he speaks gravely
but excitedly of the power of Eve's beauty. The sense of
rapture heard in his voice prepares us for the sense of
despair which we hear in Book IX, when Adam realizes
that Eve has transgressed. When he makes his great decision, he speaks in the same voice we heard in Book VIII:

> Should God create another *Eve*, and I
> Another Rib afford, yet loss of thee
> Would never from my heart; no no, I feel
> The Link of Nature draw me: Flesh of Flesh,
> Bone of my Bone thou art, and from thy State
> Mine never shall be parted, bliss or woe. (IX, 911-916)

The word *voice* best indicates these variations in *Paradise Lost*. Style is a generalized concept which suggests a
manner that is sustained without much variation, whereas
what we are concerned with is local variation in sound,
rhythm, and tone. The style of *Paradise Lost* is sublime
and elevated, but within that style there are significant
local variations. And the point that needs to be made is
that the voices of *Paradise Lost*—all of them, not just the
narrator's—and all their variations tend to establish the
values of the poem as it is read and felt as an experience.

It is quite possible to make this statement about other
narrative poems. No doubt Chaucer's Pardoner is a very
bad man, yet his charm is inescapable. We respond to his
positive joy in villainy and his happy consciousness of

himself as an accomplished villain. His energy and evident pride animate the verse in which he speaks to us. In contrast, *The Rape of the Lock* is a very proper poem if we judge it simply as a plea for restraint and acceptable social behavior. Yet underneath this surface propriety the poem is filled with insinuating sexual imagery, and it culminates in the unstated but clearly implied message that woman is merely the object of male aggression. The meaning of a complex narrative poem must be measured not only by what the words say but also by the tone of voice in which they are presented. At least it is so for modern readers. It is hard to reconcile the different tones of *Paradise Lost* with Mrs. Ferry's assertion of a single controlling voice.

What would be the consequence if one eliminated the concept of the narrator's authority and instead listened to all the different voices? Probably, to begin with, the nagging question of which voice is Milton's. For, regardless of whether one speaks of Milton or of the inspired blind bard, the fact remains that we expect some voice in the poem to be the official, authoritative voice that controls or attempts to control the whole poem. *Paradise Lost* is not a play; as a narrative it must emanate from some controlling intelligence, some point of view. One could, of course, reply that all the voices are Milton's, just as one might argue that Shakespeare speaks through all his characters. But if all the voices are Milton's, then all of them are authoritative, and where they conflict there is no way to resolve them. If, for instance, the voice in which Adam proclaims his resolve to perish with Eve is neither more nor less authoritative than the voice which later comments that they should have remembered to obey God no matter what, we are left in a kind of suspense.

Those who, like Mrs. Ferry, suppose that the voice of

the narrator controls our response to the poem will mini-
mize the conflict between the voices. The argument of
Stanley Fish is that the voices are meant to conflict, but
the voice of the narrator is certainly authoritative. The
historical scholars equate the narrator's voice with seventeenth-century Christian humanism. All these views assume that there is *a* narrator's voice, *one* voice which
speaks in its own characteristic tone. Yet it is clear that
there are many tones of voice in the poem, ranging from
the sweetness of Eve's lyric to Satan's jubilant sarcasm,
from Adam's gravely bewildered praise of Eve's beauty
to Michael's cold stoicism, from Satan's anguished soliloquy to the narrator's moralistic comments. There is a
much greater variety of tone than Mrs. Ferry's book
would lead us to believe. Even when the narrator is
speaking for himself, not giving us the words of characters in the poem, his voice varies in tone, most obviously
at those points where he comments on the action. Furthermore the voices of the characters are sometimes
nearly identical. Satan's soliloquy in Book IV sounds like
Adam's soliloquy in Book X. Eve's plea for forgiveness
in Book X reiterates the tone of the Son's intercession in
Book III. Thus the voices of the poem cannot be finally
associated with particular characters.

This complexity of tone in *Paradise Lost* lies behind the
efforts of modern scholars to establish some center of
authority in the poem—the authority of seventeenth-
century Christian humanism or of the narrator's voice
or of the supposed intentions of John Milton. But if the
reader is unable to accept this authority, he will look for
it elsewhere. To take a particular example, we may examine a passage in which we hear two different voices
and attempt to determine which is authoritative. The

passage occurs late in Book VIII, when Adam tells Raphael of the power of Eve's beauty:

> Here passion first I felt,
> Commotion strange, in all enjoyments else
> Superior and unmov'd, here only weak
> Against the charm of Beauty's powerful glance.
> Or Nature fail'd in mee, and left some part
> Not proof enough such Object to sustain,
> Or from my side subducting, took perhaps
> More than enough; at least on her bestow'd
> Too much of Ornament, in outward show
> Elaborate, of inward less exact.
>
> . . . .
>
> Yet when I approach
> Her loveliness, so absolute she seems
> And in herself complete, so well to know
> Her own, that what she wills to do or say,
> Seems wisest, virtuousest, discreetest, best;
> All higher knowledge in her presence falls
> Degraded, Wisdom in discourse with her
> Loses discount'nanc't, and like folly shows;
> Authority and Reason on her wait,
> As one intended first, not after made
> Occasionally; and to consummate all,
> Greatness of mind and nobleness thir seat
> Build in her loveliest, and create an awe
> About her, as a guard Angelic plac't.
>
> (VIII, 530–539, 546–559)

The modern reader can scarcely refrain from regarding this passage as authoritative in one sense: it states powerfully and passionately the masculine response to female beauty. No sonneteer cataloguing his mistress' physical attributes ever succeeded in conveying the power of beauty as Adam does. In view of this potent yet troubled outburst, Raphael's answer seems strange:

> Accuse not Nature, she hath done her part;
> Do thou but thine, and be not diffident
> Of Wisdom, she deserts thee not, if thou
> Dismiss not her, when most thou need'st her nigh,
> By attributing overmuch to things
> Less excellent, as thou thyself perceiv'st.
> For what admir'st thou, what transports thee so,
> An outside? fair no doubt, and worthy well
> Thy cherishing, thy honoring, and thy love,
> Not thy subjection. . . .
> What higher in her society thou find'st
> Attractive, human, rational, love still;
> In loving thou dost well, in passion not,
> Wherein true Love consists not; Love refines
> The thoughts, and heart enlarges, hath his seat
> In Reason, and is judicious, is the scale
> By which to heav'nly Love thou may'st ascend,
> Not sunk in carnal pleasure, for which cause
> Among the Beasts no Mate for thee was found.
>
> (VIII, 561–570, 586–594)

One wonders whether Raphael has really heard Adam. When the angel counsels, "What higher in her society thou find'st / Attractive, human, rational, love still . . . ," it will seem to the reader, who already has some acquaintance with Eve's charm, that Raphael is advising Adam to respond to what Adam does indeed respond to:

> those graceful acts,
> Those thousand decencies that daily flow
> From all her words and actions, mixt with Love
> And sweet compliance, which declare unfeign'd

Union of Mind, or in us both one Soul;
Harmony to behold in wedded pair
More grateful than harmonious sound to the ear.
(VIII, 600–606)

And Raphael's other suggestion,

weigh with her thyself;
Then value: Oft-times nothing profits more
Than self-esteem, grounded on just and right
Well manag'd . . . (VIII, 570–573),

confirms our suspicion that he didn't really hear Adam,
for this is exactly what Adam says he cannot do. Finally
Raphael contrasts love which "refines / The thoughts"
and "carnal pleasure," the pleasure of beasts.

It is a strange conversation. Adam seems eager to
please Raphael, and he quickly asserts that he is still free.
But Raphael has completely failed to hear what Adam
has said. He hasn't been talking about carnal pleasure; he
has been talking about Eve, not merely an outside but a
whole person, the only other person of his kind in the
whole world. The voices of Adam and of Raphael may
be called the voices of experience and of reason: Adam
relates an experience; Raphael responds as one who, having no understanding of the experience, still knows the
reasons why Adam ought not to feel that way.

Which of the two voices is authoritative? The question
does not ask which voice is John Milton's. It asks which
voice compels the reader's sympathetic response. To
which does the reader yield? Without doubt the reader
hears Adam because Adam's is the voice of human experience. What Raphael says might be good advice if any
human being could follow it. It evidently sounds good to

Adam, but he doesn't follow it. What with his blushing and his reference to being "sunk in carnal pleasure" Raphael impresses us as something of a prude.

Perhaps a good seventeenth-century Christian humanist would reply that prudery is preferable to death and damnation. If so he would be appealing not to a few lines of Book VIII but to the whole experience of *Paradise Lost*. If Adam had heeded Raphael's advice, he would not have fallen; misery and death would not have entered the world. Judged this way, Raphael's voice would seem to be authoritative: it is a part of the moral order which the epic envisions. Since that order is divinely established, Raphael as its spokesman can hardly reflect the experience of fallen humanity.

This essentially is the argument of Stanley Fish. The reader who responds with approval and sympathy for Adam has fallen into one of the traps which Milton has laid. The reader who responds to the whole grand design, on the other hand, is guided by "the truths God and Milton have proclaimed." Final authority rests with the entire pattern of the epic. No merely local effect can nullify that authority.

This seems to me to be a thoroughly responsible way to read *Paradise Lost* as long as one really sticks by it. But the one greatest temptation that one must resist is to read the poem as if one knew exactly what it says before even beginning to read it. One cannot listen to some of the voices and disregard others. As Empson puts it, "Our recent pious critics, eager to catch Satan out on a technicality all the time, must be unable to read his speeches aloud."[8] That is, they are unable to listen to Satan's voice.

8. *Milton's God*, p. 45.

C. S. Lewis gives a striking example of this kind of inability. Commenting on Eve's decision to persuade Adam to eat the Forbidden Fruit, he says, "I am not sure that critics always notice the precise sin which Eve is now committing, yet there is no mystery about it. Its name in English is Murder." [9] One could, of course, answer with an abstract and conceptual argument to the effect that murder is inconceivable to Eve, that it comes as a considerable surprise to Adam when Michael shows him the death of Abel. But no one who has listened to Eve's voice would argue that way. Eve's motives are bad enough, but her voice reveals only selfishness, self-deception, fear and doubt, not the cold-blooded determination of the murderer.

To listen to the voices of *Paradise Lost* is to respond to the poem as a felt experience. It is to recognize the variety within the poem's unity. It is to liberate oneself from preconceived patterns and expectations, whether they be based on Milton's life, Christian theology, baroque sensibility or whatever. Above all it is to realize that, although Milton addressed himself to a great task—nothing less than to provide a vision of the human condition seen, not as Shakespeare presents it in its local and temporal aspects and its sense of mystery but as the result of a great and understandable action involving Heaven and Hell— to accomplish it he had to make Heaven and Hell local and temporal. It is a mighty stage, but all the people on it are merely players. God in *Paradise Lost* is, just as Empson calls him, Milton's God. It will not help us to conclude, with C. S. Lewis, that people "who say they dislike

9. *A Preface to "Paradise Lost"* (London: Oxford University Press, 1942), p. 121.

32

Milton's God only mean they dislike God."[10] One may dislike Milton's God simply as a character in the poem. One may respond sympathetically to Satan without supposing that he is justified in his rebellion. What is in question is not our salvation but Milton's poem.

We tend quite naturally to read *Paradise Lost* as a poem which establishes its own values, not as the poetic embodiment of some dogmatic formula. For such a reading the poem's stated intention is less important than what its voices tell us. The poem will speak to us if we will listen to it—not to Milton's epic voice but to all the voices we hear in it. If we listen to the voices of *Paradise Lost* without deciding in advance what they are going to tell us, we may hear more fully what we have heretofore heard only in part—a great poem speaking directly to us.

10. Ibid., p. 126.

Formulas

3

There is very little question about what *Paradise Lost* is supposed to show. The statement of G. A. Wilkes clearly presents the orthodox understanding of the poem's grand design. "The only formula that is adequate to Milton's declared intention, and that comprehends the whole text, is that *Paradise Lost* is a treatment of the operation of Providence, traced through the celestial cycle from the revolt of the angels to the Last Judgment, and its purpose is to justify the workings of Providence to mankind."[1] The poem can be and certainly has been read according to this formula. Even the Satanists did not challenge it; they merely objected that Milton had made Satan more attractive than the formula allowed.

To particularize a bit more than Wilkes does, *Paradise Lost* is intended to show how God, after the revolt of Satan, created "our Grand Parents," placed them in a blissful garden, gave them perfect freedom, allowed them to fall into sin and eventually redeemed them. It will be noted that as soon as one gets into the particulars, some difficulties arise. One is immediately confronted with the peculiar action of God's creating a being who he knows will fall apparently so that he can then be redeemed. Such problems have been treated at length by Raleigh and

1. *The Thesis of "Paradise Lost"* (Melbourne: Melbourne University Press, 1961), p. 42.

Waldock[2] and need not be discussed at this point. But it ought to be clear that anyone who tries to reduce an eleven-thousand-line poem to a formula is going to run into trouble as soon as he applies his formula to the poem. At those points where the poem conflicts with the formula the critic can ignore the poem or falsify his response to it. What I should like to do is to read the poem insofar as possible without relying on any formula and to find its meaning from the pattern that emerges.

But where to start? The beginning of the epic is dominated by a formula that seeks to explain all of the subsequent action. It will be more practical to deal with a less inclusive statement to which some particular actions of the poem may be referred. Such a statement is included in the exchange between Adam and Raphael discussed in the preceding chapter. It deals with rising and falling, and it provides a kind of formula which may be tested by the action of the epic.

> In loving thou dost well, in passion not,
> Wherein true Love consists not; Love refines
> The thoughts, and heart enlarges, hath his seat
> In Reason, and is judicious, is the scale
> By which to heav'nly Love thou may'st ascend,
> Not sunk in carnal pleasure, for which cause
> Among the Beasts no Mate for thee was found.
> (VIII, 588–594)

It may be said, to begin with, that the distinction between love and passion is not maintained in the language of the poem. Clearly the sexual encounter immediately

2. See Raleigh, *Milton*, pp. 126–141, and Waldock, *"Paradise Lost" and Its Critics*, chap. 1.

after the Fall is not what Raphael would call love, yet the narrator says, "There they thir fill of Love and Love's disport / Took largely, of thir mutual guilt the Seal" (IX, 1042–1043). The encounter is presented as a direct result of original sin, its whole quality beautifully indicated by Adam's "now let us play." Adam and Eve evidently sink into carnal pleasure; they certainly do not ascend to heavenly love.

What is most striking about Raphael's speech, however, is its vision of the positive qualities of love, especially the relation between earthly love and heavenly love. Even without a knowledge of the Platonic thought behind these lines, the modern reader will understand them to mean that there is no absolute separation between earthly love and heavenly love. Whatever heavenly love can be seen to do for mankind, earthly love may be seen to do something of the same kind. If Raphael is right about this, then we may look for verification in the poem itself.

And, indeed, this is exactly what *Paradise Lost* shows. Heavenly love is capable of both forgiveness and sacrifice; so is earthly love. As God forgives Adam and Eve, Adam forgives Eve; as the Son offers himself as a sacrifice, Eve offers herself. The language of the poem draws attention to the parallel through the voices of the Son and of Eve. The Son says

> Behold mee then, mee for him, life for life
> I offer, on mee let thine anger fall;
> Account mee man; I for his sake will leave
> Thy bosom, and this glory next to thee
> Freely put off, and for him lastly die
> Well pleas'd, on me let Death wreck all his rage.
> (III, 236–241)

Eve pleads with Adam:

> On me exercise not
> Thy hatred for this misery befall'n,
> On me already lost, mee than thyself
> More miserable; both have sinn'd, but thou
> Against God only, I against God and thee,
> And to the place of judgment will return,
> There with my cries importune Heaven, that all
> The sentence from thy head remov'd may light
> On me, sole cause to thee of all this woe,
> Mee mee only just object of his ire. (x, 927–936)

The lines are full of echoes—"mee miserable"; "He for God only, she for God in him"; "all our woe"—which suggest that Milton intended for his readers to recall several earlier speeches, though Milton's intentions are not the point we need to see. The point is that the poem itself shows that Adam and Eve are capable of forgiveness and sacrifice, that earthly love does in fact resemble heavenly love.[3] It is as Raphael says,

> what if Earth
> Be but the shadow of Heav'n, and things therein
> Each to other like, more than on Earth is thought?
> (v, 574–576)

3. Just as earthly self-justification resembles that of Heaven:

> what could I more?
> I warn'd thee, I admonish'd thee, foretold
> The danger, and the lurking Enemy
> That lay in wait; beyond this had been force,
> And force upon free Will hath here no place.

This is Adam at the end of Book IX, but it is, both in substance and tone, very like the self-justification of God in Book III.

To the extent that earthly love resembles heavenly love it would appear that Raphael is right when he warns Adam against passion. But it may strike us as odd that this resemblance appears most strikingly at that point in the poem when Adam and Eve have alienated themselves from Heaven by Eve's injudicious eating of the Forbidden Fruit and Adam's passionate decision to die rather than lose her. In fact they haven't even repented their sin yet. The angelic guard has been recalled, God will no longer walk in the Garden, and soon the human pair themselves will be exiled. At this point they should be at their worst. Certainly they have been bad enough at the end of Book IX, and Adam reaches his lowest point in the "Out of my sight, thou Serpent" tirade. His wholesale condemnation of woman rivals God's wholesale condemnation of the human race early in Book III. So in working a reconciliation Eve seems very like the Son, taking the whole burden of guilt on herself.[4]

It is hard to avoid the conclusion that neither Adam nor Eve could have performed these acts of sacrifice and forgiveness without having committed the original sin. In their fallen state they resemble God and the Son in a way that they could not in the state of innocence. This resemblance has nothing to do with *felix culpa*, which is concerned solely with the mighty acts of God occasioned by the Fall. Adam and Eve have grown in stature and maturity because of the Fall, not in spite of it. Not in vain does God proclaim to the Heavenly Host

> O Sons, like one of us Man is become
> To know both Good and Evil, since his taste
> Of that defended Fruit. . . . (XI, 84–86)

4. See Empson, *Milton's God*, pp. 167–169, for a similar conclusion.

Not all the good is lost. Something instead is gained.

Of course the poem never says that everything was lost in the Fall. Even the rebel angels have some "virtue"— "for neither do the Spirits damn'd / Lose all thir virtue . . ." (II, 482–483). But Satan and his legions are not shown to have gained anything by their fall. In general the epic represents mankind's gains as possibilities in some remote future. Partly this is a matter of tact: we would hardly expect Adam and Eve to be rewarded for disobedience. A portion of mankind will eventually be redeemed, but only as their obedience to the voice of God makes them able to accept the freely offered gift. Yet before Adam and Eve even hear of this good news, they have already gained the capacity to act out the gestures of heavenly love.

Was Raphael then wrong? If Adam had followed the angel's advice—"weigh with her thyself; / Then value" —what would he have done? Any answer is conjectural, to be sure, but if Adam indeed is imagined to have complete freedom to choose, the conjectures will refer to possible alternatives. C. S. Lewis sees one possibility: Adam might have "scolded or even chastised Eve and then interceded with God on her behalf."[5] Stanley Fish suggests that Adam should at least have taken time to reflect before reaching his decision.[6] Irene Samuel finds, in Book III, a suggestion that Adam, like the Son, might have interceded with God for the fallen Eve. "A trust comparable to—on however lower a level than—the Son's and a self-abnegation willing to risk whatever was to be risked demanded only Adam's faith that the benevolence he had always known would remain benevo-

5. *A Preface to "Paradise Lost,"* p. 123.
6. *Surprised by Sin,* p. 269.

lent, and the whole application of the moral law might
have changed as the Son's choice changes it."[7] For Dennis
Burden the situation is not without remedy. "But the
important thing is that Adam has a remedy and Milton
of all people must know it. The remedy is divorce."[8] I
think the modern reader will be likely to agree with
Waldock: "It does not help very much to imagine what
Adam might have done; almost anything he might have
done would have been less attractive than what he did."[9]
And, interesting as it might be to propose alternate solu-
tions for Adam's problem, the biblical source offered no
alternatives for John Milton. The proper question to ask
is not what else Adam might have done but whether or
not the poem succeeds in making us see Adam's choice
as wrong. Again it is not to some formula but to a voice
that we must turn for an answer. The voice is Adam's,
and the passage is one of the most impassioned and mem-
orable portions of the entire poem.

> O fairest of Creation, last and best
> Of all God's Works, Creature in whom excell'd
> Whatever can to sight or thought be form'd,
> Holy, divine, good, amiable, or sweet!
> How art thou lost, how on a sudden lost,
> Defac't, deflow'r'd, and now to Death devote?
> Rather how hast thou yielded to transgress
> The strict forbiddance, how to violate
> The sacred Fruit forbidd'n! some cursed fraud
> Of Enemy hath beguil'd thee, yet unknown,

7. "The Dialogue in Heaven: A Reconsideration of *Paradise Lost*, III,
1–417," *PMLA*, 72 (1957), 611.

8. *The Logical Epic* (Cambridge: Harvard University Press, 1967),
p. 169.

9. "*Paradise Lost*" *and Its Critics*, p. 56.

And mee with thee hath ruin'd, for with thee
Certain my resolution is to Die;
How can I live without thee, how forgo
Thy sweet Converse and Love so dearly join'd,
To live again in these wild Woods forlorn?
Should God create another *Eve*, and I
Another Rib afford, yet loss of thee
Would never from my heart; no no, I feel
The Link of Nature draw me: Flesh of Flesh,
Bone of my Bone thou art, and from thy State
Mine never shall be parted, bliss or woe. (IX, 896-916)

Here, if anywhere in the poem, is a voice which speaks of almost unspeakable loss and desolation. There is only one alternative envisioned—utter loneliness, to which even death is preferable. Nor is it carnal pleasure that Adam cannot bear to part with but Eve's "sweet Converse and Love so dearly join'd." At this moment in the poem Raphael's talk of "self-esteem, grounded on just and right / Well manag'd" is not so much right or wrong as it is irrelevant. The experience of the poem draws us to side with Adam. There is simply nothing conceivable or revealed in the poem which we can feel he ought to do instead of choosing death with Eve. Life without her is itself a death for Adam, just as it is for Eve when she imagines "*Adam* wedded to another *Eve* . . . / A death to think."

Critics who wish to see *Paradise Lost* as true to its announced intentions will, of course, view Adam's choice in a different light. Mrs. Ferry, who is sympathetic to the power of Adam's speech, still concludes that "By choosing to follow Eve he is rejecting the possibility of 'bliss,' the state of angels in Heaven and of unfallen man in his 'blissful Paradise' (IV, 208) on earth. The choice is not inevitable; it is his sin that he chooses to think it is."[10] Stanley Fish is more severe. He points out that Adam, having heard Raphael's narrative of the War in Heaven, should have recognized the value of

> obedience founded on a base of boundless trust which is proof against the evidence of sense or reason. It is a moral he could have remembered and acted on, and on that basis we must judge him.

To this Empson would reply, "The poem somehow does not encourage us to think of an alternative plan," and Milton would say in return: true, the poem does not encourage you to think of an alternative plan, just as the situation (as it seems to be) does not encourage Adam to think of an alternative plan; but I require you to think of one yourself, drawing encouragement from an inner resource which prevails against the claims of a dramatically persuasive moment, even if the moment is one I have provided; and God requires the same of Adam. The inner resource is, of course, faith, which is what remains to Adam and the reader (and to Eve) when circumstances and their own intelligences misinform them. Faith supplies the strength of will that enables us to recall the simplicity and inclusiveness of the moral issue—God or not God—in the face of the more immediate claims of subordinate and, in some sense, illusory, issues.[11]

It is instructive to see how many critics wish to avoid the issue in Adam's choice. There is nothing illusory about it. It is simply death with Eve or desolation without her. Critical ingenuity in manufacturing alternatives is misspent. There is not the slightest hint in the poem

10. *Milton's Epic Voice*, p. 61.
11. *Surprised by Sin*, p. 270.

that Adam should scold or chastise Eve or that he should
postpone his decision to allow time for reflection (no
fear lest ardor cool?). Nor is there any basis for conclud-
ing that Eve is not irredeemably lost; the terms of the
Prohibition are not conditional, there is no escape clause.
By choosing to follow Eve, Adam is not rejecting the
possibility of bliss; he knows of no bliss that does not
include Eve.

It is indeed a hard choice, but the triumph of Milton's
art is that he makes Adam's choice so perfectly right. It is
right because it is inevitable, not in the sense that the
reader can't manufacture a half-dozen alternatives but in
the sense that the Adam Milton has created could hardly
be imagined to do otherwise. And it is no more appropriate to imagine Adam doing something else than it is to
imagine Macbeth refusing to murder Duncan. There is a
difference, of course, in that Shakespeare does show us a
Macbeth who struggles against his sin while Milton gives
us an Adam who decides almost immediately to yield.
Macbeth's struggle, however, comes early in a remarkably short play; Adam's decision has behind it the whole
weight of nearly eight thousand lines of verse, especially
those of Book VIII.

For what *Paradise Lost* shows us is that the "enormous
bliss" of Paradise springs from Adam and Eve's love for
each other. Book VIII goes to some length to make this
point inescapably clear. The Garden in which Adam
awakes is precisely the same Garden which was first described for us in Book IV. Adam finds it good, but not
good enough.

> O by what Name, for thou above all these,
> Above mankind, or aught than mankind higher,

Surpassest far my naming, how may I
Adore thee, Author of this Universe,
And all this good to man, for whose well being
So amply, and with hands so liberal
Thou hast provided all things: but with mee
I see not who partakes. In solitude
What happiness, who can enjoy alone,
Or all enjoying, what contentment find? (VIII, 357–366)

The kindly, avuncular Creator approves entirely of
Adam's desire for a consort. Nowhere else in the whole
epic does God adopt the gently teasing tone of Book VIII.
Not only does he know that Adam will want company;
he knows that what he has to offer will go far beyond
anything Adam can imagine.

What next I bring shall please thee, be assur'd,
Thy likeness, thy fit help, thy other self,
Thy wish, exactly to thy heart's desire. (VIII, 449–451)

And so it is. There is no voice of warning, no prudent
moralizer to spoil Adam's joy.

The Rib he form'd and fashion'd with his hands;
Under his forming hands a Creature grew,
Manlike, but different sex, so lovely fair,
That what seem'd fair in all the World, seem'd now
Mean, or in her summ'd up, in her contain'd
And in her looks, which from that time infus'd
Sweetness into my heart, unfelt before,
And into all things from her Air inspir'd
The spirit of love and amorous delight.
Shee disappear'd, and left me dark, I wak'd
To find her, or for ever to deplore
Her loss, and other pleasures all abjure:

When out of hope, behold her, not far off,
Such as I saw her in my dream, adorn'd
With what all Earth or Heaven could bestow
To make her amiable: On she came,
Led by her Heav'nly Maker, though unseen,
And guided by his voice, nor uninform'd
Of nuptial Sanctity and marriage Rites:
Grace was in all her steps, Heav'n in her Eye,
In every gesture dignity and love.
I overjoy'd could not forbear aloud.
　　　This turn hath made amends; thou hast fulfill'd
Thy words, Creator bounteous and benign,
Giver of all things fair, but fairest this
Of all thy gifts, nor enviest. I now see
Bone of my Bone, Flesh of my Flesh, my Self
Before me; Woman is her Name, of Man
Extracted; for this cause he shall forgo
Father and Mother, and to his Wife adhere;
And they shall be one Flesh, one Heart, one Soul.
　　　　　　　　　　　　　　(VIII, 469–499)

I don't know why Milton gives us this episode, but the
effect of it is clear enough: there is no Paradise without
Eve. The love Adam and Eve share in the Garden is not
just a facet of bliss. It is Eve's voice which makes this
clear in the most lovely passage of lyric beauty in the entire epic (see pp. 23–24). It is also perfectly clear that what
Adam and Eve share is love, not carnal passion. Adam
knows that God might create another Eve. One of the
things he might have done is to run up a list of specifica-
tions so that the second Eve would be more satisfactory
than the first, "For what God after better worse would
build?" (IX, 102) But Adam's love is for a person—not
for company, not for the female sex, but for Eve. Thus

we are not only prepared for Adam's decision; we are unable to feel that it is a wrong decision. For the poem offers us nothing else that we can call preferable.

To say that Adam's decision is right is not to imply that the reader, even the modern reader, is blind to its wrongness. The reader's response is not simple, for the poem itself is not simple. We need not quarrel with the assertion of Stanley Fish that the reader is being tested, just as Adam is being tested. But we need to see how acute Waldock's criticism is when he says that the poem too is undergoing a kind of test. If a great work of the imagination could be made to appeal solely and simply to reason and logic, we would have no problem. In terms of its logical, discursive presentation of Adam's situation, Adam is wrong. He is God's creature; his duty and joy ought to be one and the same—to glorify his Creator. By choosing death with Eve he has turned his back on God and subverted the order of the universe. We might still object, even on this level of response, that God foreknew Adam's disobedience and should therefore have made him stronger and better able to stand, though these objections are at least formally answered in Book III.

But the experience of reading *Paradise Lost* is complex. We respond not only with our senses of reason and logic but also with our feelings. When Adam makes his great decision, we both know that he is wrong and feel that he is right. If God condemns him, we cannot. One may argue, as critics have, that our sympathy for Adam arises from the fact that we too are fallen. The only problem with that answer is that it completely undermines any attempt to treat *Paradise Lost* as a work of literature. It makes possible C. S. Lewis's remark to the effect that people who dislike Milton's God simply dislike God. Milton's God is not entirely Milton's creation, to be sure, but he is a speaking character in a poem and, as such, is a fit subject for literary analysis. If we are convinced that Milton has not managed to present God in a way that would justify Adam's cleaving to Him rather than to Eve, we are merely noting a failure of Milton's imagination. If the narrator of the poem tells us that Adam ought to have obeyed God at the cost of losing Eve, we are entitled to disagree on the grounds that the narrator has already shown us an Eve who is clearly more attractive than God. This is a literary judgment based on the poem's presentation of two characters. It is not a theological proposition; it is not a metaphysical conclusion. We do not arrive at this judgment because we are fallen creatures; we arrive at it because the poem leads us to it. We should, of course, feel far more comfortable about the poem if we could agree with the narrator. We would like to agree with him. Our objections are not based on some kind of captious resentment of authority. They spring from our belief that we cannot justifiably be asked by a literary artist to deny the very responses which he himself has aroused in us.

It is clear then that in relation to the passage from which this discussion started, the poem reveals a kind of tension between Adam and Raphael which is never resolved. Raphael is right in likening earthly love to heavenly love, but Adam's love for Eve, which Raphael calls carnal passion, is not only justified but celebrated by the poetry. The narrator's formulas of prudence and rejection are simply overwhelmed by the experience of Adam and Eve's love:

> he scrupl'd not to eat
> Against his better knowledge, not deceiv'd,
> But fondly overcome with Female charm . . . (IX, 997–999)
> . . . .
> For still they knew, and ought to have still remember'd
> The high Injunction not to taste that Fruit,
> Whoever tempted . . . (X, 12–14)

What are the consequences for the poem of this tension or contradiction? Waldock puts it quite bluntly, "There is no way out. *Paradise Lost* cannot take the strain at its centre, it breaks there, the theme is too much for it." The poem asks us to condemn Adam, says Waldock, but we simply cannot condemn him, "Our predicament is this, that we are asked to set aside, to discount for the moment —not some trifling prejudice, not some new light modern fancy or custom—but one of the highest, and really one of the oldest, of all human values: selflessness in love."[12] John Peter regards this analysis as "one of those critical *aperçus* which has the absoluteness that a fact has, and can never be undermined."[13] In fact Waldock seems to me to overlook one of the most obvious truths about Adam's decision: that far from being selfless, it is utterly selfish, as Adam's voice tells us:

> How can I live without thee, how forgo
> Thy sweet Converse and Love so dearly join'd,
> To live again in these wild Woods forlorn?
> Should God create another *Eve*, and I
> Another Rib afford, yet loss of thee
> Would never from my heart; no no, I feel

12. "*Paradise Lost*" *and Its Critics*, pp. 56, 54.
13. *A Critique of* "*Paradise Lost*" (New York: Columbia University Press, 1960), p. 130.

> The Link of Nature draw me: Flesh of Flesh,
> Bone of my Bone thou art, and from thy State
> Mine never shall be parted, bliss or woe. (IX, 908–916)

This is not self-sacrifice or selflessness. Adam is simply willing to pay any price to keep Eve. He is not sacrificing himself to save her. When he says in his next speech, "to lose thee were to lose myself," he affirms what his earlier speech has already told: it is his own happiness that he is thinking of.

Now I do not think that we ought to use Adam's self-ishness as a stick to beat him with. It is no more than a sign of his humanity. We feel that his decision is right because the poem offers us no satisfactory alternative. But we must not lose sight of how profound a comment *Paradise Lost* offers us at this point: that it is possible to be utterly human and utterly right at the same time. To be sure, the narrator does not say this; the poem makes us see it, if we are willing to set aside all abstract formulas so that we can experience the poetry. *Paradise Lost* is a great affirmation of humanity, its strengths *and* its weaknesses. That is why it is a poem that still has something to say to us: because it touches our lives, our humanness.

Moreover, *Paradise Lost* continues to affirm fallen humanity beyond the passages just cited. Adam briefly notes one of the gains which the Fall has brought:

> On mee the Curse aslope
> Glanc'd on the ground, with labor I must earn
> My bread; what harm? Idleness had been worse;
> My labor will sustain me. . . . (X, 1053–1056)

This is not God's doing; it is Adam's resolute and mature acceptance of the consequences of his great decision. How telling is the curt statement of the man who, having known the unfallen bliss of Paradise, now confronts an uncertain future: "Idleness had been worse."

Further evidence of real gains that come to Adam and Eve from their fall may be drawn from the last two books. At the very beginning of Book XI the Son appears before the throne of God to present the fallen couple's prayers of repentance and to intercede for them.

> See Father, what first fruits on Earth are sprung
> From thy implanted Grace in Man, these Sighs
> And Prayers, which in this Golden Censer, mixt
> With Incense, I thy Priest before thee bring,
> Fruits of more pleasing savor from thy seed
> Sown with contrition in his heart, than those
> Which his own hand manuring all the Trees
> Of Paradise could have produc't, ere fall'n
> From innocence. (XI, 22–30)

It is true that these prayers are the products of God's prevenient grace: Adam and Eve do not accomplish their own regeneration. But the words of the Son admit of no ambiguity: the fallen pair can now please God as they could not in the Garden. The biblical precedent comes to mind, though the poem does not allude to it: "I say unto you, that likewise joy shall be in heaven over one sinner that repenteth, more than over ninety and nine just persons, which need no repentance" (Luke 15:7).

Finally, Michael, having given Adam a vision of the future, introduces a concept which would be incomprehensible to unfallen mankind:

> Only add
> Deeds to the knowledge answerable, add Faith,

> Add Virtue, Patience, Temperance, add Love,
> By name to come call'd Charity, the soul
> Of all the rest: then wilt thou not be loath
> To leave this Paradise, but shalt possess
> A paradise within thee, happier far. (XII, 581–587)

This happier paradise is not Heaven, nor is its possession directly related to the actions of God. It springs from the actions of fallen mankind, no longer obeying blindly an arbitrary prohibition but seeking to imitate the sacrificial love and clear-sighted obedience of their redeemer.

A part of the poetry of *Paradise Lost* thus envisions and dramatizes an acceptance of fallen humanity, celebrating the opportunities for growth, for an imitation of heavenly love that only the fallen state can offer. It shows us a fallen Adam and Eve who are, at the same time, more richly human and more admirable than they had been while still innocent. Their love has been tested, its strength ascertained. The world is indeed all before them and they leave the Garden hand in hand with at least the possibility that they will find the happier paradise.

But it is only a part of the poetry of *Paradise Lost* which affirms this optimistic acceptance of the human condition. As Waldock has noted, "Milton says that his theme is disobedience, and the woe that came of it. Disobedience, woe; disobedience, woe; the words are paired a hundred times in the poem."[14] The actual number of pairings is four, but Waldock is right to exaggerate. The importance of the two words in the epic is out of all proportion to the frequency of their occurrence. There is God's plenty of woe in *Paradise Lost*: murder, disease, old age, war, tyranny, tempest and flood, pestilence, treachery and perse-

14. *"Paradise Lost" and Its Critics*, p. 57.

cution. And all this woe—not some but all of it—results
from Adam's disobedience:

> In mee all
> Posterity stands curst: Fair Patrimony
> That I must leave ye, Sons. . . . (x, 817–819)

All the miseries of suffering mankind that Michael shows
to Adam in Books XI and XII, all the evils that the Litany
begs protection from, all pain and loss, every evil of whatever kind—we owe them all to Adam. *Paradise Lost* presents not the slightest waver of ambiguity on this point:
the eating of the forbidden fruit brought sin and death
and every imaginable woe into the world. Some of these
woes—discord among the elements and among the beasts
—are consequences of the original sin. But, for the most
part, Adam's sons, sharing his nature, will bring their
woes upon themselves by their own sinfulness. The diseases in the horrific catalogue (XI, 477–490) are attributed
to intemperance. Tyrants reign only over sinful men:

> Yet know withal,
> Since thy original lapse, true Liberty
> Is lost, which always with right Reason dwells
> Twinn'd, and from her hath no dividual being:
> Reason in man obscur'd, or not obey'd,
> Immediately inordinate desires
> And upstart Passions catch the Government
> From Reason, and to servitude reduce
> Man till then free. Therefore since hee permits
> Within himself unworthy Powers to reign
> Over free Reason, God in Judgment just
> Subjects him from without to violent Lords:
> Who oft as undeservedly enthral

His outward freedom: Tyranny must be,
Though to the Tyrant thereby no excuse. (XII, 82–96)

Even the good men, of whom there will be very few,
will suffer the mockery and scorn of a bad society, as the
episode of Enoch shows. The followers of the Redeemer
will be persecuted, the liberty of the Gospels subverted:

Truth shall retire
Bestuck with sland'rous darts, and works of Faith
Rarely be found: so shall the World go on,
To good malignant, to bad men benign,
Under her own weight groaning . . . (XII, 535–539)

Humanity, by and large, is a bad lot, the good man a
rarity. There will be a great deal of immoral pleasure and
tyrannical power for the bad men, but the good will
have to wait

till the day
Appear of respiration to the just,
And vengeance to the wicked . . . (XII, 539–541)

when God will raise

New Heav'ns, new Earth, Ages of endless date
Founded in righteousness and peace and love,
To bring forth fruits Joy and eternal Bliss. (XII, 549–551)

This gloomy vision of mankind and his vast potential
for sinful behavior stands in powerful contrast to the
affirmative, optimistic view presented by the treatment
of Adam and Eve. Moreover, it is a vision almost un-
modified by compassion. Adam weeps at the sight of men

tortured by disease, but Michael makes it clear that their suffering is their own fault:

> Thir Maker's Image, answer'd *Michael*, then
> Forsook them, when themselves they vilifi'd
> To serve ungovern'd appetite, and took
> His Image whom they served, a brutish vice,
> Inductive mainly to the sin of *Eve*.
> Therefore so abject is thir punishment,
> Disfiguring not God's likeness, but thir own,
> Or if his likeness, by themselves defac't
> While they pervert pure Nature's healthful rules
> To loathsome sickness, worthily, since they
> God's Image did not reverence in themselves. (XI, 515–525)

Adam weeps again at the vision of violent warfare and the plight of the one just man beset by wicked foes, though the text does not make clear exactly what arouses his compassion. The vision of the Flood draws from him "another Flood." But Michael is unmoved throughout except by righteous indignation. And the voice of Michael dominates Books XI and XII. It is very much like the voice of the Father—"Whose fault? / Whose but his own?"—and of many school teachers. "Well, I've done my best but, really, there isn't much you can do with them." The vast majority of mankind is simply written off as a bad job. They won't pay attention to their lessons; they can't even keep their margins straight. Thank goodness there are a few that make the whole thing worthwhile.

While the fall and reconciliation of Adam and Eve affirms the power of human love, Books XI and XII in the main assert two very different values: righteousness and

moderation.[15] Righteousness, exemplified by Enoch and
Noah, as Abdiel has exemplified it earlier, means fleeing
from or abandoning the unrighteous whom one is unable
to convert. Moderation or temperance may be seen as a
heroic virtue, as in Book II of the *Faerie Queene*, but even
in Spenser's handling temperance appears to be largely a
matter of rejection. To be sure, what is rejected is repre-
sented as essentially ugly and repulsive, though it is super-
ficially attractive. But as a convincing and positive virtue
moderation belongs to comedy. There is nothing very
comic about Books XI and XII of *Paradise Lost*. The last
two books show a kind of hard, rigid schematization of
the good and the bad, either singly or in the lump. The
good are simply good and they remain so, the bad likewise. The polarization is absolute.

What is the significance of all this for *Paradise Lost* as a
work of art? Is Raphael right when he advises Adam to
weigh himself with Eve, to keep a detached and rational
control over his emotions? If Raphael is right, why does
the poem make us respond positively to Adam's passionate decision? When the voices of the poem are in conflict,
we can, of course, ignore some and listen to others. By
listening only to the official speakers—God, Raphael,
Michael, and the narrator as he comments on the action
—and by assuming that because Adam and Eve are fallen
they must be wrong whenever they express sentiments
contrary to the official ones, we could see the poem in

15. The word *righteousness* is used six times in *Paradise Lost*. Four of
these occurrences are in Books XI and XII. *Moderation* appears only once
in the epic, in Book XI. The related word *temperance* occurs five times,
four times in Books XI and XII. This count is based upon John Brad-
shaw's *A Concordance to the Poetical Works of John Milton* (Hamden,
Conn.: Archon Books, 1965).

terms of a formula. Waldock, unable to do this, contended that *Paradise Lost* broke down at a crucial point.

We have observed two patterns in the epic. One is probably indicative of Milton's intentions: this is the pattern of obedience through self-control and moderation. The other is the pattern of development through trial and error. The first, imposed by divine fiat, is relatively rigid; the second allows for growth and adjustment. Books XI and XII especially affirm the authority of the first pattern. The second can be traced mainly through Books VIII, IX, and X.[16] Both patterns are *in* the poem; that is, each one is validated not because someone says it exists but because the poem shows that it exists. To the extent that we allow *Paradise Lost* to have an independent existence as a work of art which makes its own laws, both patterns are authoritative. If they conflict, the conflict cannot be resolved by appealing to something outside the poem, e.g., Milton's subconscious or seventeenth-century Christian humanism. Resolution, if it can be achieved, must be in terms of something in the poem.

My own judgment is that this resolution cannot be achieved. Perhaps it would be logical to conclude with Waldock that *Paradise Lost* breaks down, that it "cannot

16. It is given metaphorical expression in Raphael's great speech (V, 469–503). One might argue from this passage that God intended that Adam and Eve grow and change. But the terms are so vague that we can hardly imagine this development. Nor is Raphael so different from the human characters that we can see what direction the change would take. What we are given is not a blueprint but a celebration of the unity of Creation envisaged in a metaphor which suggests that growth is not only natural but that it leads to some changes which are desirable, a point which Raphael repeats in nonmetaphorical language. But for a different view see Barbara Lewalski's "Innocence and Experience in Milton's Eden," in *New Essays on "Paradise Lost,"* ed. Thomas Kranidas (Berkeley: University of California Press, 1969).

take the strain at its centre." But I cannot agree with him. Poems are not logical constructions; they obey quite another set of rules. The following chapters will, I hope, make clear how it is possible to accept the conflicts and tensions of *Paradise Lost* without reaching the apparently logical conclusion that the epic is a failure.

Freedom

4

Strangely enough, very little has been written concerning freedom in *Paradise Lost*. Given Milton's preoccupation with the defense of religious, domestic, and political freedom, one would suppose that an analysis of his great poem would be largely concerned with the concept of freedom and its importance in the poem. The word *freedom*, with the related terms *free, freely, free-will* and *liberty*, appears seventy-nine times in *Paradise Lost*. Its frequency alone suggests its importance.[1] But mere frequency is less impressive than the fact that God himself insistently proclaims the freedom of all his creatures, human and angelic.

> So will fall
> Hee and his faithless Progeny: whose fault?
> Whose but his own? ingrate, he had of mee
> All he could have; I made him just and right,
> Sufficient to have stood, though free to fall.
> Such I created all th'Ethereal Powers
> And Spirits, both them who stood and them who fail'd;
> Freely they stood who stood, and fell who fell. (III, 95–102)

Even Satan, in his anguished soliloquy on Mt. Niphates, affirms the truth of God's pronouncement, "Hadst thou

---

1. The words *obedience* and *disobedience* and their variants, e.g., *obey*, *obedient* et al., for instance, appear fifty-nine times. *Sin* and its variants occur only forty-five times.

the same free Will and Power to stand? / Thou hadst . . ."
(IV, 66–67). Raphael instructs Adam concerning his
freedom:

> God made thee perfet, not immutable;
> And good he made thee, but to persevere
> He left it in thy power, ordain'd thy will
> By nature free, not over-rul'd by Fate
> Inextricable, or strict necessity. (V, 524–528)

Adam passes this same doctrine on to Eve:

> But God left free the Will, for what obeys
> Reason, is free, and Reason he made right,
> But bid her well beware, and still erect,
> Lest by some fair appearing good surpris'd
> She dictate false, and misinform the Will
> To do what God expressly hath forbid. (IX, 351–356)

Evidently freedom may be misused. Certainly the
whole narrative of Satan's fall is designed to show the
abuse of freedom. Raphael tells of the War in Heaven in
answer to Adam's question,

> can we want obedience then
> To him, or possibly his love desert
> Who form'd us from the dust, and plac'd us here
> Full to the utmost measure of what bliss
> Human desires can seek or apprehend? (V, 514–518)

God, of course, foresees both Satan's and Adam's misuse
of freedom. What then can justify the Creator in allow-
ing his creatures to do as they please when it is clear that
what many of them please is to defy him and heap misery
on themselves?

God himself gives the answer: without freedom his creatures cannot please him by their obedience.

> Not free, what proof could they have giv'n sincere
> Of true allegiance, constant Faith or Love,
> Where only what they needs must do, appear'd,
> Not what they would? what praise could they receive?
> What pleasure I from such obedience paid,
> When Will and Reason (Reason also is choice)
> Useless and vain, of freedom both despoil'd,
> Made passive both, had serv'd necessity,
> Not mee. (III, 103–111)

Raphael says the same to Adam:

> Our voluntary service he requires,
> Not our necessitated, such with him
> Finds no acceptance, nor can find, for how
> Can hearts, not free, be tri'd whether they serve
> Willing or no, who will but what they must
> By Destiny, and can no other choose? (V, 529–534)

One would have to conclude from these passages that freedom, immensely important as it is, is not an end in itself. Its importance derives from the fact that only freedom gives meaning to obedience. But even obedience is not an end; it is a means of pleasing God. There is, then, nothing as important as pleasing God. That alone is an ultimate value for men and angels.

Lest the modern reader suppose that pleasing God is like getting in the good graces of the boss, it should be pointed out that for Milton God is "all in all." His creatures owe their very existence to Him, and they can find no true fulfillment outside of Him. To please God means

to live in the universe God has created as God intends His
creatures to live—in perfect freedom and perfect bliss.
There is no hint of obsequiousness or self-seeking in the
great concept which lies behind Milton's epic. Man can
hardly please himself unless he pleases God, for he is
God's creature and his unfallen nature is in harmony with
God's will. This is why the Book of Common Prayer
speaks of God's service as "perfect freedom."

But this great concept must be presented to the reader
in some concrete form, in terms of actions and their consequences. Therefore it is appropriate to ask what sort of
thing does please God in *Paradise Lost*. We may, in a
strictly literal way, take the epic at its word and observe
those passages in which God is said to be pleased. The
first occurs in Book III, as the Son speaks of his triumph
over Hell and the powers of darkness:

> Thou at the sight
> Pleas'd, out of Heaven shalt look down and smile,
> While by thee rais'd I ruin all my Foes,
> Death last, and with his Carcass glut the Grave . . .
> (III, 256–259)

Again it is the Son who, having received the command to
drive the rebels from Heaven, refers to God as pleased:

> this I my Glory account,
> My exaltation, and my whole delight,
> That thou in me well pleas'd, declar'st thy will
> Fulfill'd, which to fulfill is all my bliss. (VI, 726–729)

Adam recalls the words of God, spoken in response to
Adam's request for a companion: "Thus far to try thee,
Adam, I was pleas'd" (VIII, 437). No other passage in the

poem refers to God as pleased, though he apparently takes an ironic pleasure in the futile plotting of Satan and the rebels before the War in Heaven breaks out (v, 718).

Certainly these passages show that it is possible to please God. The Son's speeches suggest that God takes pleasure in active virtue, since both speeches refer to victory in combat. This is important, because Adam considers the possibility that there may not be any way to please God:

> Nor can I think that God, Creator wise,
> Though threat'ning, will in earnest so destroy
> Us his prime Creatures, dignifi'd so high,
> Set over all his Works, which in our Fall,
> For us created, needs with us must fail,
> Dependent made; so God shall uncreate,
> Be frustrate, do, undo, and labor lose,
> Not well conceiv'd of God, who though his Power
> Creation could repeat, yet would be loath
> Us to abolish, lest the Adversary
> Triumph and say; Fickle their State whom God
> Most Favors, who can please him long? Mee first
> He ruin'd, now Mankind; whom will he next?
> Matter of scorn, not to be given the Foe. (ix, 938–951)

God's own words make it clear that he is pleased by obedience. The whole episode of Abdiel's refusal to join the rebels culminates in his reception before the throne of God and the commendation, "Servant of God, well done" (vi, 29). Sometimes it pleases God to have his commands obeyed even when they can't be carried out or are quite unnecessary. His orders to the loyal angels are clear enough:

> Go *Michael* of Celestial Armies Prince,
> And thou in Military prowess next,
> *Gabriel*, lead forth to Battle these my Sons
> Invincible, lead forth my armed Saints
> By Thousands and by Millions rang'd for fight;
> Equal in number to that Godless crew
> Rebellious, them with Fire and hostile Arms
> Fearless assault, and to the brow of Heav'n
> Pursuing drive them out from God and bliss,
> Into thir place of punishment, the Gulf
> Of *Tartarus*, which ready opens wide
> His fiery *Chaos* to receive thir fall. (VI, 44–55)

Yet he makes it impossible for them to succeed, reserving that glory for the Son. And Raphael informs Adam that, on the day Adam was created, Raphael was absent from Heaven,

> Bound on a voyage uncouth and obscure,
> Far on excursion toward the Gates of Hell;
> Squar'd in full Legion (such command we had)
> To see that none thence issu'd forth a spy,
> Or enemy, while God was in his work,
> Lest hee incenst at such eruption bold,
> Destruction with Creation might have mixt.
> Not that they durst without his leave attempt,
> But us he sends upon his high behests
> For state, as Sovran King, and to enure
> Our prompt obedience. (VIII, 230–240)

God's orders may be simply tests of obedience. It is not success but obedience that counts. Gabriel and his fellows have been ordered to guard Eden:

> *Gabriel*, to thee thy course by Lot hath giv'n
> Charge and strict watch that to this happy place
> No evil thing approach or enter in. . . . (IV, 561–563)

Yet after Adam's fall the angelic guards return to Heaven only to be told that it was not possible for them to do what they had been sent to do:

> Assembl'd Angels, and ye Powers return'd
> From unsuccessful charge, be not dismay'd,
> Nor troubl'd at these tidings from the Earth,
> Which your sincerest care could not prevent,
> Foretold so lately what would come to pass,
> When first this Tempter cross'd the Gulf from Hell.
>
> (X, 34–39)

Obedience then is more than anything else a matter of submitting to God's will. Its value does not lie in the success or failure of the obedient servant but in the fact that God is pleased by it. To obey God's commands is not to know God better or to become in any way like God, nor is it necessary to understand why the commands are given. Freedom, in this scheme, is not an end in itself. It is merely a necessary condition for obedience that will be pleasing to God. The disobedient, in fact, lose the freedom that God endowed them with.

> This is servitude,
> To serve th'unwise, or him who hath rebell'd
> Against his worthier, as thine now serve thee,
> Thyself not free, but to thyself enthrall'd. (VI, 178–181)

Such servitude is entered into voluntarily. Freedom is full of risks because only the possession of it makes possible the loss of it. Once lost it is lost forever.

This is what the poem tells us about freedom. But, since a poem is also an imaginative experience, we may ask to what extent *Paradise Lost* creates in us a sympathetic response to this doctrine of freedom and obedience. Specifically we may ask whether the poem makes us feel that the highest value in its imagined world is to please God. It is not appropriate to ask how this might be done, only if it is done. The consequences of displeasing God are shown clearly enough through the gradual revelation of Satan's frustration and despair and through the vision of the future of mankind. But the emphasis on the awful consequences of disobedience hardly convinces us that there is any transcendent value in obedience. All we can see from this is that a prudent man will obey to avoid the monstrous suffering brought about by disobedience. Prudence may be a virtue but it is hardly heroic. Something more is needed, some vision of the reward for obedience that will draw out the authority of our sympathetic response.

Paradise Lost offers hints of that vision. Raphael tells Adam, in fairly vague terms, of how men may become like angels:

> And from these corporal nutriments perhaps
> Your bodies may at last turn all to spirit,
> Improv'd by tract of time, and wing'd ascend
> Ethereal, as wee, or may at choice
> Here or in Heav'nly Paradises dwell;
> If ye be found obedient, and retain
> Unalterably firm his love entire
> Whose progeny you are. (v, 496–503)

But this is not the stuff that fires the imagination. A better indication of the reward for obedience appears in the lament of the fallen Adam to whom Michael has just proclaimed the sentence of exile:

> This most afflicts me, that departing hence,
> As from his face I shall be hid, depriv'd
> His blessed count'nance; here I could frequent,
> With worship, place by place where he voutsaf'd
> Presence Divine, and to my Sons relate;
> On this Mount he appear'd, under this Tree
> Stood visible, among these Pines his voice
> I heard, here with him at this Fountain talk'd:
> So many grateful Altars I would rear
> Of grassy Turf, and pile up every Stone
> Of lustre from the brook, in memory,
> Or monument to Ages, and thereon
> Offer sweet smelling Gums and Fruits and Flow'rs:
> In yonder nether World where shall I seek
> His bright appearances, or footstep trace?
> For though I fled him angry, yet recall'd
> To life prolong'd and promis'd Race, I now
> Gladly behold though but his utmost skirts
> Of glory, and far off his steps adore. (XI, 315–333)

Here the poetry suggests what Dante shows throughout the *Paradiso:* that the highest bliss is to stand in the presence of God. This, indeed, is precisely what we are told in Book III:

> Now had th'Almighty Father from above,
> From the pure Empyrean where he sits
> High Thron'd above all highth, bent down his eye,
> His own works and their works at once to view:
> About him all the Sanctities of Heaven
> Stood thick as Stars, and from his sight receiv'd
> Beatitude past utterance. (III, 56–62)

Perhaps Milton's audience, taught that man's chief end is to glorify God and to enjoy him forever, found these hints sufficient. But the modern reader has considerable difficulty connecting Milton's portrayal of God with the idea of enjoyment. There is very little about Milton's God to suggest that anyone could take pleasure in associating with him.[2] Those who turn to *Paradise Lost* for religious truth may be able to overlook God's self-justification, his arbitrariness, his self-gratulation. But the modern reader is likely to view the poem as a work of imagination, not a compendium of divine truth. For such a reader the prospect of spending eternity with Milton's God will not be happy.

But even if the poem could convince us that pleasing God is the highest value, we would be confronted with a problem imposed by the narrative in Genesis: when Eve presents the forbidden fruit, Adam can please God only by doing nothing. Obedience to the Prohibition consists of a refusal to act. To be sure, we could say that Adam must reject the offered fruit, and Eve; but it is hard to think of rejection as a positive action. There is no other test of Adam and Eve's obedience; they can please God only by not doing something. They are free in all other respects, but their freedom is valuable only because it makes their obedience pleasing to God. Consequently their freedom exists only for them not to use it, that is, as long as they do nothing. It is an odd sort of freedom which functions only to allow one not to do something.

2. In *Milton's God* Empson has presented objections to nearly every facet of Milton's presentation of God. For a more conventional treatment, see John Peter, *A Critique of "Paradise Lost,"* pp. 9–25. For a comparison with Dante's portrayal of God, see Waldock, *"Paradise Lost" and Its Critics*, chap. 5.

If this concept of freedom as restraint and rejection were all that *Paradise Lost* had to say, we would be justified in calling it a Puritan epic. But the poem presents a totally different idea of freedom—release from restraint, opportunity to grow and develop. The words *free* and *freedom* are seldom used in the poem to signify this idea, but there is one passage that expresses it clearly.

> So Law appears imperfet, and but giv'n
> With purpose to resign them in full time
> Up to a better Cov'nant, disciplin'd
> From shadowy Types to Truth, from Flesh to Spirit,
> From imposition of strict Laws, to free
> Acceptance of large Grace, from servile fear
> To filial, works of Law to works of Faith. (xii, 300–306)

Here the emphasis is on the contrast between laws imposed from without, which is an apt description of the Prohibition, and discipline freely accepted, as Adam and Eve freely decide to live within the terms of the sentence pronounced upon them in the hope of redemption ("free acceptance of large Grace"). Just as freely, they accept the discipline of repentance and contrition at the end of Book x, offering prayers which, as we have already noted, the Son calls

> Fruits of more pleasing savor from thy seed
> Sown with contrition in his heart, than those
> Which his own hand manuring all the Trees
> Of Paradise could have produc't, ere fall'n
> From innocence. (xi, 26–30)

God has brought about this repentance, of course, but he has not imposed it upon Adam and Eve. They have accepted his grace as freely as many of their children will reject it. The Son's words clearly connect these prayers with the fruit of the Garden, but these are fruits which Adam and Eve have freely produced.

The concept of freedom which best fits the Genesis narrative is, naturally, one which emphasizes restraint and the maintenance of a static condition. If one is already living in a paradise, what is the point of change and development, which could only be for the worse? With the Fall, history begins and change becomes desirable, given the miserable conditions revealed by Michael. This makes sense as a logical pattern, but the poem is not quite so neat. As we have seen, Adam and Eve in Book x grow and develop in ways which meet with the approval of Heaven, though such growth is inconceivable in their "happy state." Even before the Fall the concept of freedom as restraint and rejection is powerfully challenged by the mother of mankind. The scene is familiar: Eve wishes to work apart, Adam warns her of the danger from their subtle enemy. Eve replies:

> If this be our condition, thus to dwell
> In narrow circuit strait'n'd by a Foe,
> Subtle or violent, we not endu'd
> Single with like defense, wherever met,
> How are we happy, still in fear of harm?
> But harm precedes not sin: only our Foe
> Tempting affronts us with his foul esteem
> Of our integrity: his foul esteem
> Sticks no dishonor on our Front, but turns
> Foul on himself; then wherefore shunn'd or fear'd
> By us? who rather double honor gain
> From his surmise prov'd false, find peace within,
> Favor from Heav'n, our witness from th'event.

> And what is Faith, Love, Virtue unassay'd
> Alone, without exterior help sustain'd?
> Let us not then suspect our happy State
> Left so imperfet by the Maker wise,
> As not secure to single or combin'd.
> Frail is our happiness, if this be so,
> And *Eden* were no *Eden* thus expos'd. (IX, 322-341)

Perhaps a good seventeenth-century Christian humanist could refute all of Eve's arguments, but Adam can't. And as one reads the passage, it is hard to feel that Eve is wrong. The poem has already celebrated, with the Abdiel episode, the triumph of faith "without exterior help sustain'd." God himself has proclaimed his creatures "Sufficient to have stood, though free to fall." When Eve asks, "And what is Faith, Love, Virtue unassay'd / Alone, without exterior help sustain'd?" we may hear this as a plea for growth, for a chance to assume responsibilities without which she and Adam will forever remain children.

For they are indeed children. They live in the world of children, the world we have all known: a world of mysterious, inexplicable commands pronounced by god-like beings who sometimes tease us but whose favor changes quickly to wrath when we disobey them. For all his quotations from Athanasius, Ambrose, and Augustine, Lewis cannot convince us that Adam before the Fall is "the sum of all human knowledge and wisdom."[3] Nor is he after the Fall, but there is no question that he is less a child after the Fall. Michael's commands, near the close of the epic, are positive. They describe an active virtue, not a passive restraint:

3. *A Preface to "Paradise Lost,"* p. 115.

> Only add
> Deeds to thy knowledge answerable, add Faith,
> Add Virtue, Patience, Temperance, add Love,
> By name to come call'd Charity, the soul
> Of all the rest: then wilt thou not be loath
> To leave this Paradise, but shalt possess
> A paradise within thee, happier far. (xii, 581–587)

This must be pleasing to God, as well as to Adam and Eve. The idea of an inner paradise is a part of the poem's justification of the ways of God to men. It suggests the value of freedom as an opportunity for growth to maturity. It does not subvert the highest stated value of the poem—pleasing God. But it does allow us to see that to please God may mean to grow as a human being rather than to remain like a child.

Thus we may discern again the tension in *Paradise Lost* between the official doctrines of the poem and its message as an imaginative experience. One voice in the poem tells us that Adam and Eve are perfectly free in a blissful paradise, that they are entirely wrong to eat the forbidden fruit, that God's grace alone makes possible some measure of recovery for their offspring. On the other hand the poem as an imaginative experience shows us that Adam and Eve lead a relatively aimless existence, enjoying a negative sort of freedom until their fall produces in them a new kind of freedom, a new maturity, and the possibility of an achievement which will surpass the purely external bliss of Paradise, although there will be an immense amount of suffering and misery for them and all their offspring.

Again we recall Waldock's comment: "*Paradise Lost*

cannot take the strain at its centre, it breaks there, the theme is too much for it." Clearly this is the point at which we need to confront this charge and answer it. It is easy to see what Waldock is getting at: if one reads *Paradise Lost* strictly in terms of its announced theme—the disobedience of mankind and God's work of redemption—the poem does not give a straightforward and unambiguous treatment to that theme. But Waldock uses an odd sort of metaphor, as if the poem were a bridge or a building whose center could be precisely located and even suffer a collapse. *Paradise Lost* is obviously not a rigid structure. The treatment of Satan clearly shows its flexibility, if one must use metaphorical terms. The Satan who speaks the anguished soliloquy on Mt. Niphates is so different from the Satan of Books I and II that we must either suppose that two different characters are appearing under one name or realize that the whole truth about Satan's character and situation is too complex to be revealed in any pat formula. Eventually we may even realize that the whole epic is about change, the greatest change that the human race has ever experienced. Obviously such a poem cannot be held within some rigid formula if it is to have any life at all. If for the richness and complexity of imagined experience we substitute formulas, we may find ourselves forced to conclude, with as sensitive a critic as Waldock, that the most movingly portrayed and richly imagined event in the entire poem is a flaw in its structure.

But, surely someone will respond, what if the formulas are *in* the poem? There must be something wrong with a poem that says it is going to do something and then proceeds to do something else. If *Paradise Lost* tells us that Adam and Eve shouldn't have eaten the forbidden fruit, why does it suggest that even without God's grace they gained a desirable maturity and were able to act in a way which recapitulates the behavior of God and the Son in Book III? Why is the kind of freedom open to fallen mankind so much more satisfying than the freedom before the Fall? Isn't *Paradise Lost* a failure on its own terms?

There may be an aesthetic which supplies the answers to such questions. It is hard to see, as a general rule, why tension and complexity and ambiguity should be desirable in a work of art, except from the point of view of critics whose profession calls for the explication of complexities. As far as *Paradise Lost* is concerned, we can only observe that the poem is all we have to go on. We cannot compare it with some nonexistent Miltonic epic poem on the Fall of Man which hews rigidly to a formula. No doubt any epic which deals with mankind, both unfallen and fallen, attempting to explain and justify the human condition, will require some degree of complexity. But, in the end, we must read and judge this particular poem. For some readers the tensions and ambiguities of *Paradise Lost* will correspond to the felt quality of life, the human condition as each person experiences it. The formulaic reading will be untrue not only to the poem itself but also to the human predicament which the poem seeks to portray and account for. Being inconsistent with itself, *Paradise Lost* can be true to the life outside it.

One clear sign of the greatness of *Paradise Lost* and of its vitality is the fact that it does speak so clearly to our age. The rigid, formulaic reading of the poem, the assertion of "the laws that grow not old," masks the truth about Milton's epic: that its complexity and ambiguity are remarkably suited to the experience of the modern reader. Every kind of faith is undergoing a severe test in our time—faith in God, in democratic government, in education, in science and technology, in due process of law, in human reason and the capability of men not to control but at least to influence the terms of their own existence. The world appears to be an inexplicable muddle. The vision of the human condition that *Paradise Lost* offers is not, of course, a muddle, but neither is it neat and abstractly logical. The most powerful impression the poem leaves is one of sad but hopeful uncertainty. Human beings, fallen or unfallen, live in the midst of mystery; it is not possible to understand either Eden or the world outside it. One must seek to please a supreme power who demands first an unquestioning obedience to an inexplicable command, then a growth in maturity and responsibility. Failure to obey brings almost unimaginable misery upon countless millions, yet there is no way to obey without denying one's nature and sacrificing the source of one's bliss. The growth in maturity is at least possible, though its reward is apparently as inexplicable as the punishment for disobedience. Eden is lost but the whole world besides is now open to the exiles. And what is the point of all this? To repopulate Heaven solely in order to deny to Satan any vestige of triumph (VII, 150–161). But the created world will fall with Adam, and the Creator knows this, so he will redeem it or at least a small portion of its inhabitants. If it were not so painful, it would be absurd. At points it does indeed touch upon absurdity: to set an angelic guard with the specific task of keeping evil out of the Garden only to tell them when they have failed that they had no chance of succeeding—what is this if not absurd?

The vision that *Paradise Lost* offers is of human beings caught in a struggle not of their own making, performing simple acts that have consequences all out of reasonable proportion, showing both nobility and meanness, and finally going out into a world which offers both pain and death but also the possibility of a paradise happier than the one they are leaving. Far from justifying the ways of God to men, the poem suggests to a modern reader that everything about them is arbitrary and inexplicable. The question of justice hardly even enters into the case. The poem is a vision of the way things are and the way they might have been. There is not much in it to make the reader feel that what might have been would be preferable. There is, instead, a great deal in it that suggests an insight into the human predicament that no formula can express. And with the insight a sympathy that we do not associate with the stern Puritan.

Those who bring to *Paradise Lost* a religious faith that lends a greater authority to the logical formulas than to the imagined experience may be satisfied with the justification of the ways of God to men. Those who can see the poem in the light of seventeenth-century Christian humanism may find precedents for Milton's development of his theme. But they will miss some of the richness of *Paradise Lost* because they will not be able to hear it. This is not to say that their interpretation of the poem will be wrong. No unique authority is claimed for the reading offered here. *Paradise Lost* is a large poem, capable of more than one interpretation. For that very reason, however, the modern reader who is not looking for divine truth or seventeenth-century humanism must be allowed his own reading of the epic. The next two chapters will develop in some detail what that reading may show.

Adam and Eve

5

Nothing is so subversive to a rigid, formulaic reading of *Paradise Lost* as the presence of Adam and Eve. They are Milton's chief triumphs, the only recognizably human figures he ever succeeded in portraying. At every turn their humanity tests the logical scheme of justification. They repeatedly shatter all the orthodox rigidities of the poem.

The matter of Adam's superiority is a good example. At the first appearance of these lords of creation, the narrator tells us that Adam is made to rule, Eve to yield:

> Though both
> Not equal, as thir sex not equal seem'd;
> For contemplation hee and valor form'd,
> For softness shee and sweet attractive Grace,
> Hee for God only, shee for God in him:
> His fair large Front and Eye sublime declar'd
> Absolute rule; and Hyacinthine Locks
> Round from his parted forelock manly hung
> Clust'ring, but not beneath his shoulders broad:
> Shee as a veil down to the slender waist
> Her unadorned golden tresses wore
> Dishevell'd, but in wanton ringlets wav'd
> As the Vine curls her tendrils, which impli'd
> Subjection, but requir'd with gentle sway,
> And by her yielded, by him best receiv'd,
> Yielded with coy submission, modest pride,
> And sweet reluctant amorous delay. (IV, 295–311)

Adam is made in the image of God, Eve in the image of Adam. Satan sees at once that Eve is his prey and does not dare to approach Adam:

> Then let me not let pass
> Occasion which now smiles, behold alone
> The Woman, opportune to all attempts,
> Her Husband, for I view far round, not nigh,
> Whose higher intellectual more I shun,
> And strength, of courage haughty, and of limb
> Heroic built, though of terrestrial mould,
> Foe not informidable, exempt from wound,
> I not. (IX, 479–487)

Raphael reminds Adam that Eve's beauty is only "An outside." Adam himself speaks the bitterest condemnation of women to be found in the poem:

> Out of my sight, thou Serpent, that name best
> Befits thee with him leagu'd, thyself as false
> And hateful; nothing wants, but that thy shape,
> Like his, and color Serpentine may show
> Thy inward fraud, to warn all Creatures from thee
> Henceforth; lest that too heav'nly form, pretended
> To hellish falsehood, snare them. . . .
> O why did God,
> Creator wise, that peopl'd highest Heav'n
> With Spirits Masculine, create at last
> This novelty on Earth, this fair defect
> Of Nature, and not fill the World at once
> With Men as Angels without Feminine,
> Or find some other way to generate
> Mankind? this mischief had not then befall'n,
> And more that shall befall, innumerable
> Disturbances on Earth through Female snares,

And strait conjunction with this Sex: for either
He never shall find out fit Mate, but such
As some misfortune brings him, or mistake,
Or whom he wishes most shall seldom gain
Through her perverseness, but shall see her gain'd
By a far worse, or if she love, withheld
By Parents, or his happiest choice too late
Shall meet, already linkt and Wedlock-bound
To a fell Adversary, his hate or shame:
Which infinite calamity shall cause
To Human life, and household peace confound.

(x, 867–873, 888–908)

Eve's final speech affirms the superiority of Adam:

Thou to mee
Art all things under Heav'n, all places thou,
Who for my wilful crime art banisht hence. (xii, 617–619)

The pattern is clear enough. Adam is like God to Eve.
Just as the highest value in the poem is to please God, the
highest value for Eve is to please Adam. She was made
precisely for that reason:

What next I bring shall please thee, be assur'd,
Thy likeness, thy fit help, thy other self,
Thy wish, exactly to thy heart's desire. (viii, 449–451)

And she does please him, so much so that upon his first
sight of her in a dream Adam is ready to leave all other
pleasures for her sake:

Shee disappear'd, and left me dark, I wak'd
To find her, or for ever to deplore
Her loss, and other pleasures all abjure. (viii, 478–480)

78

In fact, she pleases him too much, and Raphael rebukes him for his weakness. But that does not upset the established pattern; it merely suggests that Adam is not using good judgment.

Yet there are clear indications in the poem that upon some occasions Eve is at least Adam's equal, if not in fact his superior. Certainly she can be equal in both intellect and argumentative power. Her desire to work apart may indeed be based on pride and wandering vanity as Adam says, though the poem does not allow us to assess her motives. But in the argument which precedes her departure it would take a very fine scale to weigh the points on both sides to ascertain the winner. In essence Eve argues for freedom, growth, and the attendant risks; Adam argues for prudence, playing it safe, stasis. Insofar as the poem supports both points of view, both debaters are right, though our knowledge of what will happen gives Adam an advantage.

It is instructive to look at Dryden's adaptation of this debate in *The State of Innocence*. The tone of Eve's argumentation in Dryden's work allows us to appreciate more fully the persuasiveness and gravity of Milton's Eve. When Dryden's Adam asks why Eve wishes to work apart, she replies,

> Because thus warn'd, I know my self secure,
> And long my little trial to endure:
> T'approve my faith; thy needless fears remove,
> Gain thy esteem, and so deserve thy love.[1]

When Adam gives his permission, Eve says, "My Soul, my eyes delight; in this I find / Thou lov'st; because to

1. *Dryden: The Dramatic Works*, ed. Montague Summers, 6 vols. (London: Nonesuch Press, 1932), III, 448.

love is to be kind." The banality of her words ("my little trial," "to love is to be kind") contrasts with the dignity and weight of Milton's Eve. More instructive is the fact that in *The State of Innocence* Dryden has simplified the argument between Adam and Eve, making it appear that Eve's main reason for wishing to work apart is to impress Adam: "T'approve my faith; thy needless fears remove, / Gain thy esteem, and so deserve thy love." Whatever the issue is in *Paradise Lost*, it has nothing to do with impressing Adam.

Dryden's Adam muses after Eve's departure:

In love, what use of prudence can there be?
More perfect I, and yet more pow'rful she.
Blame me not, Heav'n if thou love's pow'r had'st try'd,
What could be so unjust to be deny'd?
One look of hers my resolution breaks;
Reason it self turns folly when she speaks:
And aw'd by her whom it was made to sway,
Flatters her pow'r, and does its own betray.

Dryden implies that Adam's struggle is between his prudence or reason and his love for Eve. What Milton presents is far more complex: Adam's love for Eve draws him in both directions—he fears for her safety and for her displeasure. Adam's words to Eve—"Go; for thy stay, not free, absents thee more"—are adapted in *The State of Innocence* as part of one of Eve's speeches, where they are turned into a threat:

If this shake not thy obdurate will,
Know that, ev'n present, I am absent still:
And then what pleasure hop'st thou in my stay
When I'm constrain'd, and wish my self away.

Milton's Eve needs no such threats. Her argument sustains itself except in lines 285–289 where she sounds close to the archetypal feminine resort: tears.

> His fraud is then thy fear, which plain infers
> Thy equal fear that my firm Faith and Love
> Can by his fraud be shak'n or seduc't;
> Thoughts, which how found they harbor in thy breast,
> *Adam*, misthought of her to thee so dear?

Of course one could argue that it was Eve's duty to obey Adam, that he should simply have commanded her to stay. But it is hard to see how ordinary, unadulterated authoritarianism represents superiority of any but the most arbitrary sort.

Satan's temptations can hardly be understood to prove Eve's intellectual inferiority. For one thing Satan has already seduced one-third of the Heavenly Host (a fact that Adam reminds Eve of), so he is no novice at the art. He may win Eve's attention by flattery, but it takes arguments of real substance to bring her to yield. His story is plausible to anyone who supposes that it is a serpent speaking. Eve has enough good judgment to recognize flattery (IX, 615–616), but anyone who didn't want to see the tree which produced such a wonderful effect would be intellectually dead. Her first reaction to the sight of the Tree of Prohibition is exactly right. The rest of the scene is one of Milton's triumphs. Unlike the temptation scenes between the Lady and Comus or between Satan and Christ, this scene contains no open debate. Satan makes his magnificent appeal, culminating in the master touch, "these, these and many more / Causes import your need of this fair Fruit" (IX, 730–731).

It is possible to go through Satan's speech and point out the fallacies of its argument, but the poem makes no attempt to do so. By this time the reader either sees the lies and distortions or he is no fit reader. The narrator merely comments that Satan's words are "replete with guile" and "persuasive," observations fully justified by Satan's speech. But the reader has a tremendous advantage over Eve: he *knows* who is speaking and why. Any reader who even attempts to put himself in Eve's place will realize that the poem itself does not show her to be lacking in intellect in this scene.

But, as if to make the matter unmistakably clear, the poem goes on to show us that Adam is as fully deceived as Eve. His "higher intellectual" accepts Satan's lies even when they come to him second-hand from Eve. Of course his first reaction to Eve's rather breathless outburst is right, but no more so than Eve's first reaction to the sight of the tree. And when he begins to speculate on the consequences before he eats the fruit, he is as thoroughly deceived as Eve:

> Bold deed thou hast presum'd, advent'rous *Eve*,
> And peril great provok't, who thus hath dar'd
> Had it been only coveting to Eye
> That sacred Fruit, sacred to abstinence,
> Much more to taste it under ban to touch.
> But past who can recall, or done undo?
> Not God Omnipotent, nor Fate; yet so
> Perhaps thou shalt not Die, perhaps the Fact
> Is not so heinous now, foretasted Fruit,
> Profan'd first by the Serpent, by him first
> Made common and unhallow'd ere our taste;
> Nor yet on him found deadly, he yet lives,
> Lives, as thou said'st, and gains to live as Man

Higher degree of Life, inducement strong
To us, as likely tasting to attain
Proportional ascent, which cannot be
But to be Gods, or Angels Demi-gods.
Nor can I think that God, Creator wise,
Though threat'ning, will in earnest so destroy
Us his prime Creatures, dignifi'd so high,
Set over all his Works, which in our Fall,
For us created, needs with us must fail,
Dependent made; so God shall uncreate,
Be frustrate, do, undo, and labor lose,
Not well conceiv'd of God, who though his Power
Creation could repeat, yet would be loath
Us to abolish, lest the Adversary
Triumph and say; Fickle their State whom God
Most Favors, who can please him long? Mee first
He ruin'd, now Mankind; whom will he next?
Matter of scorn, not to be given the Foe. (IX, 921–951)

Obviously he believes the Serpent's story. He too thinks of becoming a God or Angel. In his own way he is less discerning than Eve, for he reasons that even if God has seen them he will not carry out the threatened punishment. Eve at least has enough sense to know that if God has seen them they can expect to die. Adam's line of thought may be more ingenious and complicated, but it is much farther from the truth.

The scene is beautifully designed to show that although both Adam and Eve know they are going to do something wrong, they can manage to convince themselves that they are doing it for good reasons. The reasons are complex, as human reasoning is always likely to be. The complexity is part of the lasting interest of the scene. It really does no service to the poem to boil the complexity down to some simple term like trivial-mindedness or gregariousness or uxoriousness or vanity or whatever. Eve sees that they have been given an arbitrary command and threatened with a punishment that they can't begin to comprehend. The fruit may at least allow them to understand what they fear. She knows that she is supposed to be inferior even to Adam, let alone to God. She doesn't want to be inferior if she can be superior. She knows too that she may die and, if she does, she will lose Adam, so in a marvellously revealing speech[2] she decides that he must eat the fruit because she can't live without him: "So dear I love him, that with him all deaths / I could endure, without him live no life" (IX, 832–833).

Adam's reasons are simpler. He will certainly lose Eve if he doesn't partake. Perhaps the Serpent has taken the sting out of the curse, and it plainly hasn't killed him. Perhaps he and Eve will grow up to godhead; perhaps God will decide not to destroy them. But, above all, the main thing is that he cannot bear to lose Eve.

It is hard to see any intellectual superiority in Adam's line of thought. There is a distinction that needs to be noted, and it certainly shows Adam to be superior. It is, however, a moral distinction and may be simply stated: if the whole episode is seen as a competition in selfishness, Eve wins hands down. While Eve is concerned solely for herself, Adam is concerned both for himself and Eve. Eve wants Adam to die if she must; Adam wants to die if Eve must. The difference is between wanting to take what one has no right to take and wanting to give what one has no obligation to give. It is necessary to observe

2. One of the most appallingly comic speeches in all literature. It has the two necessary qualities of true comedy: it is utterly irrational and it makes good sense in context.

this, since otherwise I might give the impression that
Adam and Eve are indistinguishable in their disobedience.
The distinction is there, but it is clearly not a distinction
in intellect.

Again the contrast with Dryden's *State of Innocence* is
revealing. Just before he eats the fruit, Adam says to Eve,

> Cheat not your self, with dreams of Deity;
> Too well, but yet too late, your crime I see:
> Nor think the fruit your knowledge does improve;
> But you have beauty still, and I have love.
> Not cozen'd, I; with choice, my life resign:
> Imprudence was your fault, but love is mine.[3]

Dryden's Adam fits the formula perfectly. He really does
have intellectual superiority. Not for a moment does he
suppose that there is any escape from death or any justification for disobedience. He knows, and states quite
neatly, the nature of Eve's fault and his own. The pain,
the bewilderment, the sense of unutterable loss that
sweep over Milton's Adam do not touch him. By some
standards of judgment he may be preferable to Milton's
Adam, but the modern reader is likely to find him simply
unbelievable.

In the exchange of recriminations which closes Book
IX, there is no sign of intellectual superiority, though
when it comes to tongue-lashing Adam is no match for
Eve until his "Out of my sight, thou Serpent" of Book X.
The events of Book IX tend to support Eve's response to
Adam's attempt to put the blame on her:

> What words have past thy Lips, *Adam* severe,
> Imput'st thou that to my default, or will

3. *Dryden: The Dramatic Works*, III, 454.

Of wand'ring, as thou call'st it, which who knows
But might as ill have happ'n'd thou being by,
Or to thyself perhaps: hadst thou been there,
Or here th' attempt, thou couldst not have discern'd
Fraud in the Serpent, speaking as he spake;
No ground of enmity between us known,
Why hee should mean me ill, or seek to harm.

(IX, 1144–1152)

This is not to say that Adam never appears to be intellectually superior to Eve. No doubt he knows more than
she: he explains why the stars shine all night (IV, 660–688);
his knowledge of mental faculties helps him to comfort
Eve after her dream (V, 95–121). More impressive is his
treatment of Eve's proposals of sexual abstinence or sui-
cide. Here he is more realistic than Eve, for he realizes
that there is no way to get around the "penalty pro-
nounc't":

Doubt not but God
Hath wiselier arm'd his vengeful ire than so
To be forestall'd. (X, 1022–1024)

His speech amply justifies the narrator's reference to "his
more attentive mind" (X, 1011).

But to read the poem according to a formula which
insists that Eve is everywhere and always inferior to
Adam is to miss much of the rich humanity of both characters. Adam may be intellectually superior in Book X,
but Eve is infinitely more admirable and deserving of our
sympathy. Adam's soliloquy is an intellectual justification
of God's ways; Eve's plea for forgiveness is a passionate
act of contrition, a true offering of herself which not only
puts an end to Adam's utterly futile and, in the circum-

stances, unjustifiable recriminations, but also provides a human parallel to the action of the Son in Book III. It is not an exact parallel, for Eve acts out of her desperate need for forgiveness and, as Adam rightly says, she cannot even bear the burden of her own guilt. Like Adam's choice of death with Eve instead of life without her, Eve's offer to sacrifice herself is a complex mixture of nobility and selfishness.

It is this complexity which a formulaic reading of *Paradise Lost* masks. Yet much that Milton has invented adds to the fullness of Adam and Eve. Eve especially benefits from these additions. How could any sensitive reader of *Paradise Lost* suppose that the epic shows Milton's putative aversion to women? It is possible to judge Eve by the standards of seventeenth-century courtesy books and to find that she fails as a wife in almost every important respect.[4] Yet her charm is undeniable. Throughout the poem she is associated with flowers in a way that suggests her beauty and vulnerability. Her tenderness is implicit in her lament for the flowers she has planted in the Garden:

> O flow'rs,
> That never will in other Climate grow,
> My early visitation, and my last
> At Ev'n, which I bred up with tender hand
> From the first op'ning bud, and gave ye Names,
> Who now shall rear ye to the Sun, or rank
> Your Tribes, and water from th'ambrosial Fount?
>
> (XI, 273–279)

4. Mary Stanley Weinkauf, "The Two Faces of Eve: The Ideal and the Bad Renaissance Wife in *Paradise Lost*," Dissertation, University of Tennessee, 1966.

As she ministers naked to Adam and Raphael, her loveliness is such that the narrator remarks,

> O innocence
> Deserving Paradise! if ever, then,
> Then had the Sons of God excuse to have been
> Enamour'd at that sight. (v, 445–448)

So much in *Paradise Lost* is predicted or predictable that Eve stands out as the center of unpredictability. The odd and disconcerting dream happens to her. It is she who, out of the blue, suddenly decides that she should work apart. Perhaps no other speech in *Paradise Lost* is so fully human, so completely revealing of the ambivalences and contradictions in human feelings, as is her first speech to Adam after she has eaten the Forbidden Fruit.

It all spills out in such a rush. The first six lines are one long, breathless outburst. The excitement itself is complex: she has never lied to Adam before, yet she begins the whole speech with a lie:

> Hast thou not wonder'd, *Adam*, at my stay?
> Thee I have misst, and thought it long, depriv'd
> Thy presence, agony of love till now
> Not felt. (IX, 856–859)

But the lie culminates in what must be a truth:

> For never more
> Mean I to try, what rash untri'd I sought,
> The pain of absence from thy sight. (IX, 859–861)

She tells of the Serpent and the effects of the fruit on her. Then the lies begin again. She says that she is "growing up to Godhead,"

which for thee
Chiefly I sought, without thee can despise.
For bliss, as thou hast part, to me is bliss,
Tedious, unshar'd with thee, and odious soon. (IX, 877–880)

Like so many passages in *Paradise Lost*, this reminds us of
an earlier speech, the lovely lyric in which Eve sings the
sweetness of Paradise, and we are aware of the contrast
between the innocent honesty of unfallen Eve and the
frightened deceptions of fallen Eve. Part of the breathless
quality of this speech suggests the strength of Eve's fear
—fear that this allegedly superior being will really see
through her, that his "higher intellectual" will perceive
her lies and she will die alone. In part, too, she is trying
to convince herself: she wants to believe what she is saying and so, in a later speech, she repeats the lie but this
time in a form which reveals the falsehood more clearly:

Were it I thought Death menac't would ensue
This my attempt, I would sustain alone
The worst, and not persuade thee, rather die
Deserted, than oblige thee with a fact
Pernicious to thy Peace. (IX, 977–981)

The conclusion of this speech suggests that she has succeeded in convincing herself that there is nothing to fear:
"On my experience, *Adam*, freely taste, / And fear of
Death deliver to the Winds" (IX, 988–989). And the narrator adds,

So saying, she embrac'd him, and for joy
Tenderly wept, much won that he his Love
Had so ennobl'd, as of choice to incur
Divine displeasure for her sake, or Death. (IX, 990–993)

Far from being a point of collapse, this scene is one of the most satisfying in the whole epic. Milton has carefully refrained from flattening it out and simplifying what must be a complex experience, given the Adam and Eve he has presented in the preceding books. There is an instructive parallel in *Samson Agonistes*. Dalila comes to see Samson, offering to win his release from prison and to nurse him as a recompense for her betrayal. The offer sounds lascivious:

> Though sight be lost,
> Life yet hath many solaces, enjoy'd
> Where other senses want not their delights
> At home in leisure and domestic ease,
> Exempt from many a care and chance to which
> Eyesight exposes daily men abroad. (914–919)

But there is no reason to suppose that she doesn't really want to care for Samson. The scene consists mainly of his accusations and her apologies. When Samson finally refuses even to let her touch his hand, Dalila explodes into anger and exults in the fame she will enjoy among the Philistines as the woman who saved her country. As she leaves, the chorus remarks, "She's gone, a manifest Serpent by her sting / Discover'd in the end, till now conceal'd" (997–998).

The trouble with the scene is that the remark of the chorus is not justified by Dalila's behavior. She is, as far as we can tell, honestly seeking a reconciliation with Samson. His intransigent rejection of all her attempts drives her to take a position as angry and rigid as his has been. The significance of the scene is blurred primarily because we don't know enough about Dalila. The conclusion of the chorus corresponds with but a small portion of what we have seen. It is only by assuming that no Philistine can do anything right that we can agree with the chorus that Dalila is a serpent. But Eve's behavior when she offers the Forbidden Fruit to Adam corresponds perfectly with everything we know about her: her fear of death, her need for Adam, her capacity for self-deception, her real love for Adam. No wonder she weeps for joy when he accepts the proffered fruit. It is a natural, human thing to do. Nor does the narrator suggest that Eve's tears are specious. The scene avoids any kind of narrow formula. Even the narrator's comment, that Adam was "fondly overcome with Female charm," is blurred by the pun on *fondly* and by the very real charm of Eve as the poem has presented her.

Waldock argues that "the Fall transmutes [Eve] into a woman, a person; one by one the human lineaments are etched in before our eyes."[5] Certainly the Fall confirms the impression we have formed of Eve, but she is a person from her very first appearance. Her portrait is made of numerous small touches. For example, when Adam perceives Raphael approaching the Bower, he asks Eve to prepare food for the angel:

> But go with speed,
> And what thy stores contain, bring forth and pour
> Abundance, fit to honor and receive
> Our Heav'nly stranger; well we may afford
> Our givers thir own gifts, and large bestow
> From large bestow'd, where Nature multiplies
> Her fertile growth, and by disburd'ning grows
> More fruitful, which instructs us not to spare. (V, 313–320)

Instead of leaving at once, Eve answers:

5. *"Paradise Lost" and Its Critics*, p. 62.

> *Adam*, earth's hallow'd mould,
> Of God inspir'd, small store will serve, where store,
> All seasons, ripe for use hangs on the stalk;
> Save what by frugal storing firmness gains
> To nourish, and superfluous moist consumes:
> But I will haste and from each bough and brake,
> Each Plant and juiciest Gourd will pluck such choice
> To entertain our Angel guest, as hee
> Beholding shall confess that here on Earth
> God hath dispenst his bounties as in Heav'n. (v, 321–330)

Milton's intention in this punning exercise remains in doubt, but the effect of Eve's speech may be assessed. It suggests a sort of independence in her: she will obey Adam, not unwillingly, but she wants him to understand that she knows about household matters. She will give the heavenly visitor the best the Garden has to offer because that is part of her role in the economy of Eden. She can do this without officious suggestions from Adam. There is a touch of rebuke in her reply, as if she were saying, "This is my business; just let me handle it." When, in Book IX, she suggests a real change in the economy of the Garden and argues stubbornly with Adam, we are seeing a full-scale projection of the qualities which are merely hinted at in this brief exchange.

Eve's very first speech is another example of the complexity of her character. She recalls her first conscious moments:

> That day I oft remember, when from sleep
> I first awak't, and found myself repos'd
> Under a shade on flow'rs, much wond'ring where
> And what I was, whence thither brought, and how.
> Not distant far from thence a murmuring sound

Of waters issu'd from a Cave and spread
Into a liquid Plain, then stood unmov'd
Pure as th'expanse of Heav'n; I thither went
With unexperienc't thought, and laid me down
On the green bank, to look into the clear
Smooth Lake, that to me seem'd another Sky.
As I bent down to look, just opposite,
A Shape within the wat'ry gleam appear'd
Bending to look on me, I started back,
It started back, but pleas'd I soon return'd,
Pleas'd it return'd as soon with answering looks
Of sympathy and love; there I had fixt
Mine eyes till now, and pin'd with vain desire,
Had not a voice thus warn'd me, What thou seest,
What there thou seest fair Creature is thyself,
With thee it came and goes. . . . (IV, 449–469)

Milton's adaptation of the Narcissus story delicately suggests Eve's tendency to vanity. Later, in Book IX, Satan will play quite blatantly, and successfully, upon that very tendency.

As Eve's reminiscence continues, we are able to see another important aspect of her character: her pliability. She recalls her first sight of Adam:

What could I do,
But follow straight, invisibly thus led?
Till I espi'd thee, fair indeed and tall,
Under a Platan, yet methought less fair,
Less winning soft, less amiably mild,
Than that smooth wat'ry image; back I turn'd,
Thou following cri'd'st aloud, Return fair *Eve*,
Whom fli'st thou? whom thou fli'st, of him thou art,
His flesh, his bone; to give thee being I lent
Out of my side to thee, nearest my heart

> Substantial Life, to have thee by my side
> Henceforth an individual solace dear;
> Part of my Soul I seek thee, and thee claim
> My other half: with that thy gentle hand
> Seiz'd mine, I yielded, and from that time see
> How beauty is excell'd by manly grace
> And wisdom, which alone is truly fair. (IV, 475–491)

Eve's yielding to Adam suggests her pliability, as her first turning away implies that she has to learn, "How beauty is excell'd by manly grace / And wisdom, which alone is truly fair." She has learned this lesson, to judge by her words. The whole point of her speech is to affirm her consciousness of her

>   happier Lot, enjoying thee
> Preeminent by so much odds, while thou
> Like consort to thyself canst nowhere find. (IV, 446–448)

Yet it may not be too subtle to see in this invented episode a suggestion that in the deepest part of her being Eve loves herself because that is her nature.

Later in the epic Adam tells Raphael about his first sight of Eve and his earnest pursuit of her. Adam's account is significantly different from Eve's recollection. In Adam's version, when first he saw Eve she was approaching him,

> Led by her Heav'nly Maker, though unseen,
> And guided by his voice, nor uninform'd
> Of nuptial Sanctity and marriage Rites. (VIII, 485–487)

He does not mention Eve's pool-gazing. Upon seeing him, she turned. We know why, because Eve has already told Adam why: she preferred her own image to his manly grace. But that is not what Adam tells Raphael:

> She heard me thus, and though divinely brought,
> Yet Innocence and Virgin Modesty,
> Her virtue and the conscience of her worth,
> That would be woo'd, and not unsought be won,
> Not obvious, not obtrusive, but retir'd,
> The more desirable, or to say all,
> Nature herself, though pure of sinful thought,
> Wrought in her so, that seeing me, she turn'd;
> I follow'd her, she what was Honor knew,
> And with obsequious Majesty approv'd
> My pleaded reason. (VIII, 500–510)

The two accounts are separated by some 3000 lines of narrative, and we cannot tell whether Milton intended the discrepancy. But the effect of comparing these recollections is to suggest that Adam prefers to know, or at least to tell, something other than the full truth about Eve. It is all right for her to tell him that at first she preferred her own image, but either it isn't the sort of thing he wants Raphael to know or Adam himself doesn't want to know it. So he gives a quite different explanation of her conduct. He has prepared this explanation by saying that Eve is not "uninform'd / Of nuptial Sanctity and marriage Rites," when the fact is that she has never seen a man or heard of marriage. That is the fact, at least, if we accept Eve's account as honest, which we do because she has no conceivable reason for making up a story so clearly unflattering to her.

The problem is to estimate how much weight to put on this odd discrepancy. It is certainly less obtrusive than the ringing pronouncements of Raphael, who sternly warns Adam about Eve's "shows." It is less obtrusive than open confession of his passion for Eve, though Adam's account of Eve's creation leads logically and naturally to that confession. But it should not go unnoticed, for it subtly reinforces our impression of Adam as a man deeply troubled by *his* awareness of a discrepancy, or rather several discrepancies all of which have to do with Eve. One is stated quite openly in Book VIII: that he finds it very difficult to feel superior in Eve's presence.

> Yet when I approach
> Her loveliness, so absolute she seems
> And in herself complete, so well to know
> Her own, that what she wills to do or say,
> Seems wisest, virtuousest, discreetest, best;
> All higher knowledge in her presence falls
> Degraded, Wisdom in discourse with her
> Loses discount'nanc't, and like folly shows;
> Authority and Reason on her wait,
> As one intended first, not after made
> Occasionally; and to consummate all,
> Greatness of mind and nobleness thir seat
> Build in her loveliest, and create an awe
> About her, as a guard Angelic plac't. (VIII, 546-559)

Another discrepancy is that this subordinate creature not only has a mind of her own, but she perversely uses it to oppose him and reject him. The rejection is implicit in her preference for her own image, the opposition and rejection in her desire to work apart. But the largest, most fundamental discrepancy is that, for Adam and Eve, Paradise *is* their love for each other, yet that love is so constituted that it is not consistent with a long continuance in the Garden. This we may take as implicit in

Adam's troubled words to Raphael which draw an absolute contrast between Eve and everything else in the Garden:

Thus I have told thee all my State, and brought
My Story to the sum of earthly bliss
Which I enjoy, and must confess to find
In all things else delight indeed, but such
As us'd or not, works in the mind no change,
Nor vehement desire, these delicacies
I mean of Taste, Sight, Smell, Herbs, Fruits, and Flow'rs,
Walks, and the melody of Birds; but here
Far otherwise, transported I behold,
Transported touch; here passion first I felt,
Commotion strange, in all enjoyments else
Superior and unmov'd, here only weak
Against the charm of Beauty's powerful glance. (VIII, 521-533)

The relation between Adam and Eve is qualitatively different from all the rest of Paradise. It subverts the order of the Garden: it disturbs the certainties meant to calm the mind. It is doing Satan's work before he enters the Garden, and it heals and reconciles before the intervention of God's grace. It is a compound of selfishness and sacrifice, weakness and strength. *Paradise Lost* may be less than satisfying in its portrayal of divine love, but no other poem in the English language presents as comprehensive and sympathetic a treatment of human love. It covers the full range from bliss to misery, from affection and courtesy to hostility and rejection. It is the image of that "apt and cheerful conversation" which was, for Milton, the essence of a true marriage, and it presents briefly but vividly a portrait of the poignant suffering that comes from being "entangl'd with a pois'nous bosom snake."

Neither Heaven nor Hell, Adam and Eve's love is a paradigm of the middle state of mankind, with its attendant ambiguities and confusions. To read *Paradise Lost* without demanding that it correspond to a rigid formula is to recognize the relation between Adam and Eve for what it is: the chief glory of the poem, the portion which speaks most directly and profoundly to the modern reader.

Satan

6

Satan's role in *Paradise Lost* is clearly defined: he is the Serpent who tempts Eve and, through her, Adam to commit the Original Sin. This is what Book I tells us and what the poem shows us.

> Who first seduc'd them to that foul revolt?
> Th'infernal Serpent; hee it was, whose guile
> Stirr'd up with Envy and Revenge, deceiv'd
> The Mother of Mankind. (I, 33–36)

In a formulaic reading of *Paradise Lost* one finds no difficulty in accommodating Satan. In spite of the comments of the Satanists, he is far less subversive to the stated meaning of the poem than are Adam and Eve. The good that comes to Adam and Eve because of the Fall is none of Satan's doing. Envy and a desire for revenge drive him to seduce Eve. Guile is his most obvious weapon. Nearly every statement he makes can be seen either as a lie or a delusion. He is much more convincingly bad than God is good.

Yet there are oddities about Satan as Milton presents him. They do not suggest that Satan is admirable or good or that Milton was of the Devil's party without knowing it. But they give us the impression that Milton, whether intentionally or not, went far beyond the needs of his theme in developing Satan's character. The magnificent rebel of Books I and II—the military leader, the accomplished politician, the daring explorer—is already complex enough on the surface. The disdainful revenge seeker of Book I, the commander whose voice alone gives hope and renewed life to his followers, becomes in Book II the clever manipulator of parliamentary action and, in the scene with Sin and Death, the smooth, dissembling hypocrite. This, in itself, is a fair range of character even though we see it only from the outside. But when we reach the soliloquy in Book IV, we realize that the fallen angel who has shown insuperable determination, "considerate pride," and infernal guile is torn by remorse and a desire for reconciliation. The splendid outside conceals a turmoil within.

The speech begins in a voice that we can easily associate with Satan as he has been presented in Books I and II. Disdain, envy, and hate animate the first seven lines.

> O thou that with surpassing Glory crown'd,
> Look'st from thy sole Dominion like the God
> Of this new World; at whose sight all the Stars
> Hide thir diminisht heads; to thee I call,
> But with no friendly voice, and add thy name
> O Sun, to tell thee how I hate thy beams
> That bring to my remembrance from what state
> I fell, how glorious once above thy Sphere. (IV, 32–39)

But the next two lines could hardly be expected: "Till Pride and worse Ambition threw me down / Warring in Heav'n against Heav'n's matchless King." The phrase "Heav'n's matchless King" may mean simply that no one can defeat God in battle, but it suggests that Satan admires God and it prepares us for the complete collapse of Satan's proud defiance in the following lines:

Ah wherefore! he deserv'd no such return
From me, whom he created what I was
In that bright eminence, and with his good
Upbraided none; nor was his service hard.
What could be less than to afford him praise,
The easiest recompense, and pay him thanks,
How due! (IV, 42–48)

What follows is an anguished attempt to shift the burden of guilt from his own shoulders.

O had his powerful Destiny ordain'd
Me some inferior Angel, I had stood
Then happy; no unbounded hope has rais'd
Ambition. Yet why not? some other Power
As great might have aspir'd, and me though mean
Drawn to his part; but other Powers as great
Fell not, but stand unshak'n, from within
Or from without, to all temptations arm'd.
Hadst thou the same free Will and Power to stand?
Thou hadst: whom hast thou then or what to accuse,
But Heav'n's free Love dealt equally to all? (IV, 58–68)

Critics who enjoy pointing out Satan's lies and fallacious arguments will find little to work with here. The rebel, puzzled and remorseful, tries to understand his own behavior. It is a powerful and impressive performance, not least because it conveys so vividly the torment of knowing simultaneously that one is wrong and that one must go on being wrong. After this soliloquy there is no need for the narrator to tell us that Satan is "rackt with deep despair," for the anguished twisting and turning of his mind convey despair in a way that his first speech in Book I, instinct with driving energy and defiance, does not.

Because of its power, the soliloquy has a considerable effect on the character of Satan. Obviously it makes his character more complex. We see for the first time that behind the impressive facade of defiance and ambition, Satan knows that he is wrong. Perhaps, put in such flat terms, the statement does not show its full implications. Satan knows he is wrong—not that he has made a mistake, not that he has suffered a temporary setback—he knows that he is wrong. His pride is wrong, his defiance is wrong, his ambition is wrong: everything that defines him is wrong. Such knowledge is torment enough, but in addition Satan knows that there is no way for him to get right, and he knows why. Those who enjoy finding all kinds of sin embodied in Satan will point out that he is, in this soliloquy, preeminently guilty of despair. But God himself has made it clear that there is no hope of mercy for the fallen angels:

> The first sort by thir own suggestion fell,
> Self-tempted, self-deprav'd: Man falls deceiv'd
> By th'other first: Man therefore shall find grace,
> The other none. (III, 129–132)

Satan is enough of a realist to know that he is forever fallen. Moreover he blames his fall on no one but himself:

>   but other Powers as great
> Fell not, but stand unshak'n, from within
> Or from without, to all temptations arm'd.
> Hadst thou the same free Will and Power to stand?
> Thou hadst: whom hast thou then or what to accuse,
> But Heav'n's free Love dealt equally to all?

It is a remarkably honest admission, for it undercuts absolutely every public utterance that Satan has made in Books I and II. This is not to say that all Satan's previous utterances are lies. Some are evidently delusions, and the delusions persist. In this soliloquy he still hopes to get some kind of power and reign as a rival of God, which is all that Beelzebub, as Satan's spokesman, proposed in the "great consult." He doesn't know that God has

> Left him at large to his own dark designs,
> That with reiterated crimes he might
> Heap on himself damnation. (I, 213–215)

But he does know that the throne of Hell brings only torment, that there is no hope of respite, ever.

The responses elicited by this soliloquy are complex and various. We might simply feel that Satan is receiving the punishment he deserves. We might be drawn to sympathize with a character who faces so honestly the fact of his own responsibility for his sufferings; such an honest admission of guilt ought to count for something. We might be tempted to wonder why God denies his grace to the fallen angels, thus driving them to despair and attempts at revenge which will ultimately damn the human race.

But, whatever our response is, we will see that the effect of this soliloquy is to add depth to Satan's character, to give him a kind of inner life which is consistent with our own sense of inner life. Unlike Sin and Death, who are flat allegorical figures, Satan is portrayed as having a conscience and an inner being which can hardly fail to remind us of the same qualities in Adam and ourselves. We may conjecture that Satan's soliloquy in Book IV is consciously intended to parallel Adam's soliloquy in Book x, that the two soliloquies show us vividly and concretely how the consciousness of being wrong results in despair until, as in Adam's case, the remembrance of the Son's words brings hope of redemption.

This does not imply that Satan is a realistically presented character. Like Shakespeare's Richard III, Satan is capable of making a conscious choice of evil, a choice which no human being can conceivably make. But his soliloquy allows us to see what is not so clear in his earlier speeches: that he knows his course is evil and takes it only because it is impossible for him to relent and sue for grace, not because he finds joy or fulfilment in evil. When he declares, "Evil be thou my Good," we are aware of a complexity in those words: they are modified by what has preceded them. Evil cannot be good for Satan, as he knows; but all good is lost to him. Evil is all he has, all he can live by. It is his choice in the sense that neither his own nature nor God will let him choose anything else.

The consequences for *Paradise Lost* are that its vision of evil, after Satan's first soliloquy, becomes enfeebled. This is not the same thing as saying that *Paradise Lost* shows evil to be impotent. Books XI and XII attempt to show the real power of evil in human history. But after Satan's soliloquy it is clear that as an *agent* of evil Satan is nearly helpless. Not only can he do only what Heaven permits, but he is torn by a realization of his own weakness. He finds Adam and Eve so attractive that he could love them,

> so lively shines
> In them Divine resemblance, and such grace
> The hand that form'd them on thir shape hath pour'd.
>
> (IV, 363–365)

His powerful speeches of Book I deal with revenge and the unconquerable will to hate. By Book IX he has found not only that revenge is bitter but that the word *revenge* is not even the proper term for what he hopes to accomplish.

> Revenge, at first though sweet,
> Bitter ere long back on itself recoils;
> Let it; I reck not, so it light well aim'd,
> Since higher I fall short, on him who next
> Provokes my envy, this new Favorite
> Of Heav'n, this Man of Clay, Son of despite,
> Whom us the more to spite his Maker rais'd
> From dust: spite then with spite is best repaid.
>
> (IX, 171–178)

Spite is the word Satan himself uses; it is a shriveled, small-minded, weak man's form of revenge. The archangel whose tremendous passion dominated Book I has now become like an angry child.

This development fits neatly enough into the logical pattern of the poem. God is indeed omnipotent; consequently evil has no power of its own. The angel who fought in Heaven can no longer contend with a mere man. As Rajan has pointed out,[1] Satan's weakness is no less a part of the seventeenth-century view than is his apparently great power. He can do no harm to anyone who does not first yield to his blandishments. So the vision of Books XI and XII conveys to us again and again that the sufferings of men are their own fault. All Satan's designs are frustrated and evil becomes the work of bad men.

One wonders what Milton would have made of the Lisbon earthquake or of the atomic bomb. For the mod-

---

1. *"Paradise Lost" and the Seventeenth-Century Reader*, pp. 97–98

ern reader's experience of evil is not nearly so rational as Milton's scheme prescribes. It is more in accord with the Shakespearian visions of evil in *Macbeth* and *King Lear*, with Coleridge's *Rime of the Ancient Mariner*, or most compellingly with Kafka's nightmares, *The Trial* and *The Castle*. This may be because the modern reader has no faith in God or in the Christian religion. Whatever the reason, it would be immensely difficult to equate the staggering evils of our time—the threat of nuclear holocaust, the facts of racism and starvation, the brutalization of countless millions, the facelessness of great cities, the relentless poisoning of air and water—with a simple formula that blames these evils on individuals who cannot within reason find themselves responsible for their own sufferings or those of their fellow men. The obvious fact to the modern reader is that these evils possess an overwhelming power. It is simply not possible to connect them with anything as rational as Satan. Air pollution, for instance, has something of the irrationality of Coleridge's genie who pops up out of a well and insists that he must kill a merchant because a date shell the merchant had cast into the well has put out the eye of the genie's son. The ordinary individual simply cannot see himself as responsible for making the air unfit to breathe. If Milton's Satan had plotted to pollute the air, he would first have lamented the necessity of doing so devilish a trick, then justified it on the grounds that he was merely doing to men what God had already done to the fallen angels, and upon returning to Hell he would have found the air more noxious than ever.

By making Satan a person, a rational being who justifies his attacks upon mankind and pities his own fallen state, Milton has envisioned a kind of evil—conscious, purposeful, aware of its own nature, evil with a conscience, evil despairing of rest or joy or victory. The problem for the modern reader is that he cannot envision the modern experience of evil in these terms. Evil for us is impersonal and vast, no more purposeful than a glacier and no more selective than an atomic bomb. We are naturally Manichaeans. To recognize this is not to attack Milton's art. We could hardly expect him to be a Manichaean. It is merely to note that his poem does not speak to us powerfully of the nature of evil as we have experienced it.

But if *Paradise Lost* does not present a vision of evil as an independent and awesome power, it does show us another aspect of evil: it shows us how Satan is *in* us, not outside us. The metaphysical evil that engulfs Macbeth and all Scotland, the evil that is always known by its otherness, its total estrangement from humanity, is no part of Milton's vision. Nor should it be in the universe of *Paradise Lost*. If the root of all sin is disobedience and if there is no evil which is not the consequence of disobedience, then evil is conceivable only in human terms—in terms, that is, of conscious choice.

> O Woman, best are all things as the will
> Of God ordain'd them, his creating hand
> Nothing imperfet or deficient left
> Of all that he Created, much less Man,
> Or aught that might his happy State secure,
> Secure from outward force; within himself
> The danger lies, yet lies within his power:
> Against his will he can receive no harm.
> But God left free the Will, for what obeys
> Reason, is free, and Reason he made right,
> But bid her well beware, and still erect,

Lest by some fair appearing good surpris'd
She dictate false, and misinform the Will
To do what God expressly hath forbid. (IX, 343-356)

In the last analysis, conscious evil of this sort is always irrational. C. S. Lewis has given an excellent analysis of Satan's predicament, the "doom of Nonsense," as he calls it.[2] It is certainly no accident that Adam and Eve fall into exactly the same fallacies as Satan or that Adam's soliloquy in Book x reminds us so strongly of Satan's soliloquy in Book IV. But Satan shows us sin in a way that Adam cannot—sin in its essence, the absolute will to disobedience. About the origin of evil Milton tells us nothing, but he makes clear the terms of its continuance —unrelieved suffering and despair for the sinner. Behind the splendid facade and real power of evil, we see the shrunken, tortured plotter, denying his own nature (created good, he is naturally drawn to Adam and Eve) but unable to deny what his intellect clearly tells him—that spite, not revenge, is the end of his endeavors. The modern reader is not likely to see Satan as an ass. Instead he will see the fallen Archangel as a bundle of contradictions —a helpless menace, evil in spite of his nature, suffering in his moment of triumph, "only Supreme / In misery." It is impossible to hate such a being; it is inconceivable that anyone would wish to be like him. But neither will anyone fear him. When he slinks away after beguiling Eve, he ceases to have any further role in the poem; unlike the Devil, a less dignified being, Satan has no more work to do among men. The references to him in Books XI and XII prefigure his defeat. His punishment by metamorpho-

2. *A Preface to "Paradise Lost,"* chap. 13.

sis seems gratuitous, for Milton has so humanized Satan that there is only one appropriate punishment for him: to be Satan.

Our final impression of Satan is that he is above all futile. It is no small trick to have caused the Fall of Man, to have brought Sin and Death into the world. But to do so with no hope of ever regaining what was lost, in the knowledge that a full and satisfying revenge is forever denied—this is indeed to chew the bitter ashes of defeat. While Milton may not have succeeded in showing that obedience to God's will brings joy and fulfillment, he has given us in Satan a powerful demonstration of how futile disobedience is.

The consequences for the reader are clear enough. Beginning with Satan's soliloquy in Book IV, *Paradise Lost* suggests that evil has no power of its own. Its agents are human beings. Even diseases depend upon human intemperance. In every age there will be a multitude of bad men. They, and not Satan, will persecute the elect. The good man will be isolated, as Abdiel, Enoch, and Noah are lone defenders of the faith, but by obedience he will win God's approval. It is a remarkably simple and reasonable arrangement, suggesting that life is a process of making choices—to obey or not to obey. And the choices are perfectly clear. Evil is easily identifiable; the good man stands out in his goodness. Salvation, it is true, depends upon the redeeming work of the Son, but the entire narrative of his life on earth occupies slightly over one hundred lines, a tiny portion of the whole vision of the future. The general impression one gets from Books XI and XII is that all of mankind can be divided into two groups—the sheep and the wolves, the righteous and the wicked. It is the simplicity of this vision that makes these last two books difficult for even so enthusiastic a Miltonist as C. S. Lewis to appreciate. The problem is not that Books XI and XII present us an "untransmuted lump of futurity,"[3] but that the experience of Adam and Eve is rich and complex while the vision offered by Michael is relatively bare and simple. And nothing else in *Paradise Lost* is as complex as Satan. Adam and Eve are exactly what they appear to be; Satan's circumstances force him to play different roles. After the soliloquy in Book IV, we are fully aware of the suffering his hypocrisy causes him. According to the formula that God states, Satan's suffering is his own fault in a way that Adam's is not. But the experience of the poem is rather different. To seventeenth-century readers, perhaps any temptation could be attributed directly to Satan. But the text of the poem clearly implies that the wicked act without the intervention of Satan and without his agonized sense of guilt. By dividing the entire human race into the bad and the good, the poem has abandoned the insights offered by the complex experience of Satan and of Adam and Eve. Instead it gives us a simple scheme: the good, isolated and few in number, will suffer from the scorn and persecution of the great bad majority. The trouble with Books XI and XII is not that the future is untransmuted but that the past is undigested—the immediate past, including Satan's experience of guilt and the suffering it brings, likewise the ambivalence of Adam and Eve's ordeal; in short all of the poem which escapes from the straitjacket of formula into the sanity and perilous freedom of life.

3. Ibid., p. 125.

Milton's treatment of Satan fits easily into the formula of his epic, but his powerful and imaginative vision of Satan, together with Adam's experience of guilt, renders Michael's revelation of the future rather bare and lifeless. In Satan the *sense* of guilt is unforgettably portrayed; in Books XI and XII we see only the *fact* of disobedience.

John Milton

Having banished John Milton so rigorously from his epic in order to make it ours, we owe him the courtesy at least of justifying his exile. Why should this great poem be read as if its author had no rights in it? Are not his life and his other writings a commentary of sorts on his masterpiece? Don't we run the risk of distorting his achievement by arbitrarily separating it from his life and work?

Certainly one ought to admit the possibility of distortion. *Paradise Lost* is only a part of Milton's work. Other works reflect better certain facets of his mind and his art. For our purposes, however, it is not Milton's mind but his poem that we are concerned with; nor is it all of his art but just that portion visible in *Paradise Lost*. His skill in handling the Italian sonnet or his mastery of Jonsonian octosyllabic couplets is in no way relevant to his epic. Actually the risk of distortion is much greater when we assume that *Areopagitica* or *De Doctrina Christiana* or Milton's experiences in Cromwell's government or his difficulties with Mary Powell can in some way be used to interpret his epic. The problem is always where to draw the line. Milton's learning was prodigious. Perhaps he had read Juan Gonzalez de Mendoza's *Historie of the Great and Mighty Kingdome of China* in Robert Parke's translation and thence derived his knowledge of Chinese wind-wagons.[1] Did he intend that his readers recall that the Latin root of the name Mendoza means *prevarication*? Are we therefore to assume that Milton was skeptical of the wind-wagon story? Why then did he refer to wind-wagons? We get into tangles of this sort when we try to interpret *Paradise Lost* by referring to Milton's reading or to his experiences or even to his other writings.

It is tempting, for instance, to read *Paradise Lost* in terms of *Areopagitica*. After all, the oration has a great deal to say about freedom, about choosing between good and evil, about Adam's free will, about active and mature virtue. When E. M. W. Tillyard did just this, he came to the conclusion that Satan "wins our profoundest sympathy and admiration" because "it is Satan who in *Paradise Lost* best expresses that heroic energy of Milton's mind, best hitherto expressed in *Areopagitica*, which undoubtedly, though in very different form, would have been the master emotion of the projected Arthuriad."[2] The use of *Areopagitica* as a commentary of *Paradise Lost* not only leads Tillyard to an untenable statement about our attitude toward Satan; it also opens the way for a positive description of a work which doesn't even exist. The fact is that *Areopagitica* can tell us nothing useful about *Paradise Lost*. Milton himself made it clear that his oration dealt with fallen mankind: "As therefore the state of man now is; what wisdome can there be to choose, what continence to forbeare without the knowledge of evill?"[3] But, more to the point, *Areopagitica* is an argu-

1. Frank L. Huntley, "Milton, Mendoza, and the Chinese Land-Ship," *Modern Language Notes*, 69 (June 1954), 404–407.

2. Tillyard, *Milton*, pp. 278–279.

3. *Works*, IV, 311.

ment, not a vision. It is the work of a controversialist, not that of a poet.

In fact there is very little in Milton's poetry or prose which even vaguely foreshadows *Paradise Lost*. What Milton's earlier work lacks is precisely that dimension of human sympathy which so enriches his epic. Nothing prepares us for the characterization of Satan, for instance. We might hope to find some anticipation of the Adversary in the "Acheronte tyrannus" of *In Quintum Novembris*. But though this creature is called "fraudumque magister" and though he counsels the Pope to work through fraud, he is quite unlike Satan. He is what Satan fails to be—a force of evil at work among fallen men, stirring up war and discord. He has no inner being at all. The same is true of Comus. He is far too joyous, too positive in his evil. Though he can tempt the Lady with a magnificently sensuous celebration of *carpe diem*, compared to Satan he is inept in the selection of time and place. And he lacks both the grandeur of the earlier Satan and the misery of the later. The Satan of *Paradise Regained* is simply another character. Several thousand years of history have taught him that he is God's servant: "For what he bids I do" (I, 377). With the loss of his pride he has lost his grandeur: "This wounds me most (what can it less?) that Man, / Man fall'n, shall be restor'd, I never more" (I, 404–405). He is so utterly humbled and futile that he can tell us nothing about the role of Satan in *Paradise Lost*. Neither before nor after the Satan of *Paradise Lost* did Milton present us anything like him.[4]

4. Perhaps the sonnet "On the Late Massacre in Piemont" suggests something of Satan's fierce hunger for revenge. What it does not suggest is that such righteous indignation can be coupled with a sense of guilt.

Adam and Eve, Milton's supreme achievement, are utterly without parallel in English literature, let alone in Milton's writings. Unlike the Lady in *Comus*, who is a speaking abstraction, Eve is delightfully human, full of contradictions, weak enough to commit the original sin, strong enough to offer her life as a sacrifice for Adam. Adam, curious and troubled, overwhelmed with gratitude for this creature that he doesn't know how to control, willingly tasting death to remain with her, is obviously no Arthurian hero, no Sir Guyon either. There is simply nothing in Milton's work outside of *Paradise Lost* that can give us any insight into these two characters. They are the greatest celebration in English poetry of the love of husband and wife—steadfast, forgiving, consoling, enduring. The divorce tracts try to define this kind of love, but it is by Adam and Eve that we gain an understanding of what Milton referred to in his prose, not the other way around.

As for *De Doctrina Christiana*, attempts to explicate *Paradise Lost* in terms of Milton's creed can only succeed in masking the qualities which make the epic different from all the rest of Milton's writing. It is interesting to find in *De Doctrina* that Milton regarded the Son as subordinate to the Father, but generations of orthodox Christians read the epic without ever suspecting this heresy. How then is the treatise relevant to the poem? *De Doctrina* tells us that the eating of the Forbidden Fruit was a compendium of all kinds of sin. The epic does not show this or even suggest it.

Even the verse of *Paradise Lost*, the only aspect of the poem that Milton ever commented on, is inexplicable on the basis of his earlier poetry or anybody else's. He had proved himself an absolute master of rime—in the sonnet, in eight- and ten-syllable couplets, in his own stanza forms, in exquisite songs and in the intricate, extended harmonies of *Lycidas*. Then he turned his back on it, "Rime being no necessary Adjunct or true Ornament of Poem or good Verse, in longer Works especially, but the Invention of a barbarous Age, to set off wretched matter and lame Meter." As for blank verse he had used it in *Comus* with all the skill one would expect of a great poet, but the blank verse of *Comus* gives no hint of the far more sonorous and powerful verse of *Paradise Lost*.

The events in Milton's life form the least reliable basis for an understanding of his epic. This is so precisely because we have *in* the poem everything that Milton thought we needed to have to understand it. But there is a great deal that we do not know about John Milton. Is Eve a reflection of Mary Powell? If so then Mary Powell was a rare woman indeed. Is Adam a picture of John Milton in his domestic bliss or discontent? Was Milton unable to present God sympathetically because God is pictured as a king and Milton hated kings? Is the saving sacrifice of the Son played down because Milton disliked the idea of needing a mediator? Is the parliamentary procedure in Hell a reflection of Milton's distrust of Parliament? The questions, as one can easily see, are all backwards. That is, they lead from observable facts about *Paradise Lost* to speculations about John Milton.

Indeed many of the qualities of *Paradise Lost* which speak most directly to the modern reader are without precedent in Milton's earlier writing and, as far as anyone can tell, in his life. All the earlier poetry has a tendency to move away from human beings in favor of an idea or an ideal. Only "L'Allegro" and "Il Penseroso" establish a human scale, and they are idealizations. The Holy Family is barely in the "Nativity Ode." The characters in *Comus*, though involved in a human problem, are mostly concerned with philosophical disputation. The human Edward King becomes the idealized shepherd Lycidas. As for the prose it is utterly given over to ideas and arguments. Only in the divorce tracts does Milton deal with a problem that must be faced as a complex issue requiring attention not to some ideal but to a relationship between human beings. In the prose tracts we encounter the dogmatic, argumentative, sarcastic Milton—the controversialist who is totally convinced that his side only is right and that his opponents are a pack of mercenary scoundrels. What is lacking in all of Milton's writing before *Paradise Lost* is the ability to enter sympathetically into the mind and experience of any human being, including himself, without reaching out irritably for simple answers to complex problems. He altogether lacked negative capability. For every problem there must be a clear-cut solution. How many of the lines we recall most readily from his poems are essentially answers to questions:

> All is, if I have grace to use it so,
> As ever in my great task-Master's eye.

. . . .

> Virtue may be assail'd but never hurt,
> Surpris'd by unjust force but not enthrall'd,
> Yea even that which mischief meant most harm
> Shall in the happy trial prove most glory.

. . . .

> But that two-handed engine at the door
> Stands ready to smite once, and smite no more.

. . . .

New Presbyter is but *Old Priest* writ Large.

. . . .

They also serve who only stand and wait.

Only once outside *Paradise Lost* did Milton simply present an experience of pain and loss for which he envisions no solution whatsoever: "But O, as to embrace me she inclin'd, / I wak'd, she fled, and day brought back my night."[5] The figure who appears in his dream may be idealized, but the sonnet speaks of an irrecoverable loss, both of the beloved wife and of the speaker's own vision. There is no solution in the poem; he must live in the situation with only the trust of having "Full sight of her in Heaven without restraint." The poem answers no questions, though the poignant sense of deprivation certainly raises some. Sonnet XXII is more typically Miltonic as it confronts his blindness with the question, "What supports me, dost thou ask?" and responds with the clear and simple answer:

> The conscience, Friend, to have lost them overplied
> In liberty's defense, my noble task,
> Of which all Europe talks from side to side.

What makes *Paradise Lost* so different from all the rest of Milton's work is the tension between the clearly enunciated, logical analysis of the Fall and Redemption of man on the one hand, and the sympathetic response to dilemmas that, because they cannot be resolved, must simply

5. For another treatment of the relation between Milton's life and his poetry, see Thomas Wheeler, "Milton's Twenty-third Sonnet," *Studies in Philology*, 58 (July 1961), 510–515.

be lived in, either despairingly or hopefully, and to human values that cannot be made to fit the logical analysis. The formula by which the ways of God to men are to be justified provides a logical interpretation of the events in the poem. But there are many episodes which the formula does not call for, episodes which set up another kind of pattern: Eve's recollection of her creation, Adam's conversation with God before the creation of Eve, his troubled awareness of the power of her beauty, the debate about working apart, Eve's offer of herself to satisfy God's wrath, Adam's speech of reconciliation with Eve, the whole development of Satan's tortured inner being—these and many other small touches show Milton responding sympathetically and imaginatively in a way that no one could have predicted from his earlier poetry. This part of *Paradise Lost*, the part that speaks most directly to the modern reader, is that portion which appertains to the deepest humanity in John Milton. One can only speculate on what produced this unexpected development in his art. He had come to know defeat and bitter disappointment, irrecoverable loss, and perhaps a sense of hopelessness—the very experiences that are met by Satan, Adam, and Eve. But his life is closed to us while his poem stands open, a testimony to the strength of hope and affirmation in a blind man who could produce a splendidly articulated epic of nearly eleven thousand lines. Our only responsibility is to respond to it, neither as Milton's earlier poetry suggests nor according to our knowledge of seventeenth-century theology, but according to the art of the poem as we are capable of seeing it. For the art of *Paradise Lost* is the part of John Milton's life which still lives for us, "the precious lifeblood of a master spirit, embalmed and treasured up on purpose to a life beyond life."

Our Epic

8

Paradise Lost lives for us in the same way that any literary masterpiece must: by entering our lives. It is we, in fact, who make it live. Milton's metaphor speaks of embalmed blood. The scholar who sees *Paradise Lost* as an artifact which preserves the theology or philosophy or literary preoccupations of the seventeenth century will wish to think of the poem as an inviolable corpse, beautifully preserved and set in a museum for our reverent inspection, or as a monument protected from unclean hands by a very high fence. We may be more nearly satisfied with Proust's metaphor. "But I say that it is the cruel law of art that human beings should die and that we ourselves must die after exhausting the gamut of suffering so that the grass, not of oblivion but of eternal life, may grow, the thick grass of fecund works of art, on which future generations will come and gaily have their 'picnic lunch,' without a thought for those who sleep beneath."[1] This suggests a continuing life, not the artificial preservation of something long since dead. But Proust's metaphor is not quite right; it is too resolutely aesthetic, as if a work of art were merely to be enjoyed and then abandoned. To be sure, it is no small matter to be for countless readers a refuge and a place of joy. Nevertheless *Paradise Lost* continues to be much more nearly what Milton intended it

1. *Remembrance of Things Past,* trans. Frederick A. Blossom (New York: Random House, 1934), IV, 390.

to be—an embodiment of truth, even of saving truth. Not perhaps the truth that Milton intended to convey, but a truth that is central to our time.

It is this truth that makes it possible for us to give life to *Paradise Lost*. We could not lend it our life unless it truly touched our life. I do not know any metaphor for this other than that of communion. We feed on literary masterpieces because they nourish us, because they are life-giving. But we do not all, or always, hunger for the same thing. Our hunger is an expression of our needs, which vary from one age to another. Great works of literature truly live in us, but only because we have incorporated them. And our capacity to do this depends both on what they can offer us and what we need.

This is not a doctrine of pure subjectivism. Literary masterpieces do in fact have the capacity to feed our hunger. But it is also a fact that our needs vary. Wilson Knight, turning to *Paradise Lost* in the desperate days of 1941 when England stood alone against Germany, read Milton's epic as a poem about war, and he specifically related it to the war in which England was engaged. "Satan's legions attend their leader like hordes of black-uniformed Nazis gathered in their thousands by the illumination of interlacing searchlights to hear Hitler speak at Nuremberg. The cries of 'Sieg Heil!' thundering heroic resolution have their counterpart in *Paradise Lost*." The War in Heaven resembles the war in Europe. "Such is the battle before the advent of Messiah. It may, according to my scheme, be allowed to correspond roughly with our present world-conflict at the moment of writing (May 1941); a conflict of accepted good, trust in God, and certain natural alliances, against aspiring will-to-power and cunning use of mechanised resource." Knight works out this comparison in more particular detail. "The good angels resemble Great Britain in that they have no further ambitions, and are defending what they believe, on the whole, to be a God-supported order, with the righteousness of their cause nevertheless profiting little against explosives; while the others resemble our foes in point of heroic determination, mechanical invention, and a bold over-leaping of moral canons, with a partly justifiable sense of wronged worth in face of what they consider absurd injustice."[2]

We cannot see the poem this way, but the point is that in 1941 *Paradise Lost* was alive for Wilson Knight and it spoke in a way that was immediately relevant to the English people. The situation defined their needs—for an affirmation of the righteousness of their cause, for a great imaginative vision of truth embattled and hard pressed to hold the field, for a prophecy of victory. We cannot today read the War in Heaven as Knight did. Our needs are so different that we can hardly respond to Book VI at all except by reading it as a parody or a satire.

Nor should we be blind to the dangers inherent in Knight's method. He has, in effect, made propaganda out of a great epic. He has reduced its scope and narrowed its vision. And, without doubt, any attempt to relate *Paradise Lost* to the needs and concerns of a particular place and time must court that danger, whether the place and time be England in the 1660s or the United States in the 1970s. Yet, I think, the attempt must be made. Joseph Summers has put the case so clearly that it is worth repeating his statement. "It is, I think, *our* great heroic poem. Perhaps some of our difficulties arise from the fact

2. *Chariot of Wrath: The Message of John Milton to Democracy at War* (London: Faber and Faber, 1942), pp. 143–144, 149, 151.

that we have seen it too exclusively as a poem which looks to the past, to an alien antiquity, and not sufficiently as one which looks also as firmly and unmistakably towards the future. Perhaps . . . we have not boldly enough taken possession of it as our own."[3] To take possession of *Paradise Lost* as our own does not mean that we will enlist its support for any cause. Certainly we will not make it a vehicle for propaganda. We will simply ask in what ways the poem speaks to us in our own time and place.

Because *Paradise Lost* is a great poem it does speak to us. It responds to our needs and enters our lives. At least for the people of the United States in the 1970s *Paradise Lost* deals with the most difficult and agonizing problem of our time: the problem of change, of an old order and a new. It is not a measure of the poem's value that it does so, not insofar as its value is judged by literary or historical standards. But its relevance is a measure of its value to us and of our right to read it on our own terms.

"The old order changeth, yielding place to new." So says the dying Arthur. It's a fairly easy thing for a dying man to say: he doesn't have to live with the new. Sir Bedivere is a better spokesman for us:

> But now the whole ROUND TABLE is dissolved
> Which was an image of the mighty world;
> And I, the last, go forth companionless,
> And the days darken round me, and the years,
> Among new men, strange faces, other minds.

In every facet of our national life the old order is changing and we are not sure what, if any, order will take its place.

3. "The Embarrassments of *Paradise Lost*, in *Approaches to "Paradise Lost*," ed. C. A. Patrides (Toronto: University of Toronto Press, 1968), pp. 75-76.

What could better exemplify the old order than the neighborhood school, the one center of concern for all the families of the neighborhood? Around it are clustered all the aspects of order which most profoundly affect our society: the sense of community, the promise of children, the measured and even process of schooling, lasting friendships, graduation, and the beginning of mature life. But all the old assurances embodied in the neighborhood school are under attack. And whether we think that the attacks are justified or not, we are aware that a new order now coming into existence may require a different kind of school and even a whole new concept of what a school exists to do.

The problem of order which we can see in the challenge to the neighborhood school is felt more poignantly in the family. For here order is most closely related to our deepest feelings and there is no resort to law when order breaks down. The so-called youth culture of our time is, in many respects, a calculated affront to the values of parents—cleanliness, respect for private property, an aggressive will to succeed in the race for material possessions, a belief in the righteousness of the United States.

On the national level the old order is challenged everywhere—in colleges, in courtrooms, in the streets by demonstrators and by police who are hired to control them, by laws which strike at the old order and by criminals who care for no order, by youths who desecrate the flag and by angry patriots who assault the flag-burners.

In what way can a poem published three hundred years ago speak to a society which is being torn apart today? Certainly not by answering questions. *Paradise Lost* can hardly solve our domestic and international dilemmas. Great literature does not exist to answer our questions.

Neither does it enable us to forget them. What it gives us instead is a flight of imagination which allows us to see our problems in the perspective of humanity. It speaks to us as members of the human family and defines our humanity for us, not by lecturing but by showing, enacting. The basis for our communion with literature is this common humanity by which we lend it our life in exchange for its power to bring order and significance into our life.

Paradise Lost both speaks to us of order and enacts order. As we have already seen, the poem envisions two kinds of order—that which God establishes as good and that which grows out of the humanity of Adam and Eve. God's order is relatively fixed and unchanging; within it men may "turn all to spirit" and ascend to a heavenly paradise, and Adam's descendents will come to Eden "From all the ends of th'Earth, to celebrate / And reverence thee thir great Progenitor" (XI, 345–346). This is the concept of order that looks to the past for a great beginning. It celebrates memory rather than change, conservation rather than growth. It allows much but what it forbids is absolutely prohibited. Its keynote is obedience. But look what it offers in return for obedience: immortal life, enormous bliss, the assurance of approval and reward.

The other kind of order is harder to define because it is hinted at in the poem, not developed in detail. In essence it is an order that grows out of conflict. It looks to the future rather than to the past. It celebrates a self-imposed discipline and a sense of responsibility. Its keynote is reconciliation. Because it is an internal order, it really has nothing to offer but the paradise within, the state of wholeness.

Paradise Lost speaks to us of both of these kinds of order. It insists on the gulf between God and men. God's order was good, was meant for men's good. But men could not live in it, for they saw their own good through their own eyes. The Son acted to reconcile men to God, to make possible the new order and the paradise within, which the Son's earthly life exemplified. The poem holds these two concepts of order in balance,[4] not finally rejecting either but attempting to reconcile them by showing that both are validated by acts of God. The closing lines show just how beautifully these two concepts of order can be balanced.

> They looking back, all th'Eastern side beheld
> Of Paradise, so late thir happy seat,
> Wav'd over by that flaming Brand, the Gate
> With dreadful Faces throng'd and fiery Arms:
> Some natural tears they dropp'd, but wip'd them soon;
> The World was all before them, where to choose
> Thir place of rest, and Providence thir guide:
> They hand in hand with wand'ring steps and slow,
> Through *Eden* took thir solitary way.

Nine lines perfectly balanced on the fulcrum of the fifth line. The first four look back to the order of the past, the lost beginning. The last four look ahead to the future, to the order that Adam and Eve already carry within them and to the world in which that order may be established, not without struggle. The fifth line mediates between the

4. In an uneasy balance, it must be added. Most of Books XI and XII and many of the narrator's comments suggest that the reader is expected to react negatively to the second kind of order, though it is never totally rejected. Furthermore there are some connections between this kind of order and Satan's rebellion. Indeed there could hardly fail to be, since Milton has deliberately paralleled Satan's rebellion and Adam and Eve's disobedience. But Satan stands out against the essential element of reconciliation which defines the second kind of order.

two orders—sorrow for the loss of the old order, and hope that makes the sorrow endurable.

The poem enacts the same balance between two kinds of order. The order of the past, the great beginning, is the order embodied in epic: the beginning in the middle of things, the scenes of combat, the great set speeches, the mingling of human and divine, the epic similes and elevated diction. The other order is *sui generis:* a heroic poem without a hero, the whole action turning on a domestic quarrel and the eating of a piece of fruit, told by a narrator who openly expresses his scorn for the traditional heroic poem. And the end of the poem is also a beginning.

Certainly *Paradise Lost* speaks directly to us. We too are caught between an idea of order which looks back to primal innocence and simplicity, and a new order which the human needs of our times are calling into existence. Nowhere is this seen more clearly than in our colleges and universities. The old image of the campus as a place of quiet detachment, cut off from the problems of society, a place where students sit at the feet of learned men and drink in wisdom (among other things) until, upon graduating, they go out to meet the responsibilities and struggles of the world—this image has been irreparably shattered. A society which, like ours, is torn between two orders will find an affirmation in *Paradise Lost,* an affirmation of life lived in the tension between the old and the new, an affirmation of hope and reconciliation. Both in form and content *Paradise Lost* is a celebration of what is lost and what is yet to be gained. Not a pure celebration: it will not do to claim that much. Clearly there is a strong current of rejection in the poem, and that too will speak to modern readers, for none of us can view the new order without a sense of fear and rejection. And in celebrating what is lost there is a failure of imagination, an inability on Milton's part to make us believe in that "enormous bliss." But though the poem pulls against itself, it does not ultimately deny either of the orders it envisions.

This is not to say that *Paradise Lost* has anything to do with ideas of progress. Adam and Eve do not progress: they fall, and in their fall something is lost forever. To be sure, something also is gained—a maturity and responsibility that they did not have before—but it can never replace what is lost. The new order can be reconciled with the old; it can even be seen in terms of the old, the "paradise within thee, happier far." But the "happier far" aspect of the paradise within is in the future—a hope, not a present reality.

Nor should *Paradise Lost* be construed as saying that there is right on both sides, that both the old and the new must reach some kind of compromise. The poem deals with life and death, not matters of opinion. Far from showing how differences of opinion can be resolved, it proclaims that in the midst of death there is life. It does this in theological terms in Book III when the Son offers himself as a ransom for mankind. But it does it more powerfully in human terms when, in Book X, Adam and Eve, reconciled to each other, turn from death to the life that is before them.

Life doesn't just grow out of death. It is achieved by an act of faith. It involves pain and struggle. And it carries within it that very death which it sprang from. *Paradise Lost* itself embodies this message. Much of what was dead or death-dealing in John Milton survives in his epic: the fierce hatred of Roman Catholicism, the Puritan emphasis on prudence and rigid restraint, the sense that life is properly lived according to fixed rules, the conscious assertion of masculine superiority. But Milton never lost faith in the central affirmation of his great poem: that in the midst of loss and pain there is life. Out of the wreckage of his hopes for England, in his blindness, expecting that fit readers would indeed be few, he created a work which lives for us today. Perhaps he wrote better than he knew, but that too is an act of faith.

Not much faith is required of us. Only enough to sustain us in the belief that a great work of literature always speaks to us of our own life. Of course it tells of another time and another place, another set of beliefs and assumptions. But it is not alive for us until it touches the time and place we live in. *Paradise Lost* can do this, not because we believe that we all descend from Adam and Eve but because Milton's Adam and Eve illustrate our humanity; not because we believe in Satan but because we know the torment of guilt and the burning need to assuage it. We may not believe in Eden, but we have all experienced something like it and we know the pain of loss. A great deal of *Paradise Lost* is dead for us, just as a great deal of Homer and Dante and Shakespeare is dead. But in the midst of this death there is life, not the fictitious life of a galvanized corpse but the real life that touches our life. And our business is with life.

Selected Bibliography

The following are some books which are especially important in the general study of *Paradise Lost*.

Broadbent, J. B. *Some Graver Subject*. London: Chatto and Windus, 1960.

Burden, Dennis. *The Logical Epic*. Cambridge: Harvard University Press, 1967.

Bush, Douglas. *Paradise Lost in Our Time*. Ithaca: Cornell University Press, 1945.

Daiches, David. *Milton*. New York: Hutchinson's Universal Library, 1957.

Empson, William. *Milton's God*. London: Chatto and Windus, 1961.

Ferry, Anne. *Milton's Epic Voice*. Cambridge: Harvard University Press, 1963.

Fish, Stanley. *Surprised by Sin: The Reader in Paradise Lost*. New York: St. Martin's Press, 1967.

Hyman, Lawrence. *The Quarrel Within: Art and Morality in Milton's Poetry*. Port Washington, N.Y.: Kennikat Press, 1972.

Lawry, Jon. *The Shadow of Heaven*. Ithaca: Cornell University Press, 1968.

Lewis, C. S. *A Preface to Paradise Lost*. London: Oxford University Press, 1942.

Peter, John. *A Critique of Paradise Lost*. New York: Columbia University Press, 1960.

Rajan, Balachandra. *Paradise Lost and the Seventeenth Century Reader*. London: Chatto and Windus, 1947.

Raleigh, Walter. *Milton*. New York: Putnam, 1900.

Ricks, Christopher. *Milton's Grand Style*. Oxford: Clarendon Press 1963.

Steadman, John. *Milton's Epic Characters*. Chapel Hill: University of North Carolina Press, 1968.

Stein, Arnold. *Answerable Style*. Minneapolis: University of Minnesota Press, 1953.

Summers, Joseph. *The Muse's Method*. London: Chatto and Windus, 1962.

Tillyard, E. M. W. *Milton*. London: Chatto and Windus, 1930.

Waldock, A. J. A. *Paradise Lost and Its Critics*. Cambridge: Cambridge University Press, 1947.